ACTION RESEARCH FOR EDUCATORS

Daniel R. Tomal

Rowman & Littlefield Education
Lanham • New York • Toronto • Oxford

This title was originally published by ScarecrowEducation. First Rowman & Littlefield Education edition 2005.

Published in the United States of America
by Rowman & Littlefield Education
A Division of Rowman & Littlefield Publishers, Inc.
A wholly owned subsidiary of The Rowman & Littlefield Publishing Group, Inc.
4501 Forbes Boulevard, Suite 200, Lanham, Maryland 20706
www.rowmaneducation.com

PO Box 317
Oxford
OX2 9RU, UK

Copyright © 2003 by Daniel R. Tomal

British Library Cataloguing in Publication Information Available

Library of Congress Cataloging-in-Publication Data

Tomal, Daniel R.
    Action research for educators / Daniel R. Tomal.
        p. cm.
"A ScarecrowEducation book."
Includes bibliographical references and index.
    ISBN 0-8108-4613-6 (pbk. : alk. paper)
    1. Action research in education—United States—Case studies. 2. Group work in education—United States—Case studies. I. Title.
LB1028.24 .T66 2003
370' .7'2—dc21

                                                    2002012991

CONTENTS

PREFACE

Action research is one of the most practical and efficient methods of conducting research by educators. The mere mention of the word "research" should not bring terror to the minds of educators. Many educators feel that conducting research is too complicated, painstaking, and time consuming. However, action research can offer a viable approach for conducting meaningful and practical research for school improvement.

This book has been written based upon years of study, research, and in-service training workshops on this topic. The strategies have been applied in both public and private elementary and secondary schools and in university settings. This book includes many proven principles and ideas for teachers and administrators. *Action Research for Educators* is based on a collaborative approach of recognizing the needs of all educators in utilizing a simple but powerful method of conducting research within the educational environment.

The concepts of action research can be used to support any educational program. It is a practical and no-nonsense approach that can be used by any educator—early childhood, elementary and secondary, pre-service teacher programs, in-service teacher development programs, and at the graduate university level in educational research courses. Action research is a viable model that can be used by all educators in solving educational problems and making school improvements. Action research can also be fun and satisfying for an educator who collaborates with colleagues and students in finding solutions to problems.

The first chapter provides the principles and nature of educational research. It describes the differences in quantitative and qualitative research methods and how action research is different than these traditional methods. The chapter concludes with a definition and description of action research and how it is commonly used today in business and education.

Chapter two is a crucial chapter in that it provides a history of action research and a working model of this methodology. It gives the steps that an educator can use to conduct action research. The chapter also describes how to develop a formal action research proposal, conduct a literature review, and benchmark. The chapter concludes with basic ethical and legal considerations and guidelines when conducting research.

Chapter three is a detailed chapter that provides several methods of collecting data. The chapter provides an overview of several strategies for data collection, such as: observing, interviewing, surveying, assessing, and processing.

Chapter four is important because it explains how to analyze data and make interpretations in a practical manner. It presents basic statistics in a logical and easily understandable approach, especially for people who hate statistics. The chapter also explains how to guard against threats to validity, construct meaningful graphs and diagrams using basic Microsoft Excel, and how to write narrative reports.

The fifth chapter explains how to actually solve problems through action research. It describes several barriers to problem solving, steps in solving problems, managing change, and planning and initiating action.

The sixth chapter describes how to evaluate and follow up on actions. It covers areas to evaluate, methods for evaluating results, and following up on the results of actions.

The last chapter presents an actual published action research study with a detailed commentary so that you can follow the steps to the action research model and develop a similar action research study. For those of you ready to start conducting action research, appendix A lists seventy-five ideas for conducting action research studies. These practical and viable ideas could be used by any educator to conduct action research and make educational improvements.

FEATURES OF THE BOOK

Many books written on educational research can be dry, esoteric, and impractical for educators. This book is unique because it presents clearly defined examples and content that is practical and user-friendly for all educators. The most intriguing and unique feature of this book, unlike other books written on research, is the introduction of well-defined procedures in conducting action research for both teachers and administrators. Also, understanding the use of several techniques can allow educators to rapidly employ these techniques in their own educational environment. The use of action research can help teachers improve discipline, motivate students, increase student learning, student self-esteem, and quality of school life in their classroom. For the school administrator, action research can help improve: attendance, discipline, teacher morale and performance, communications, parent and community relations, student performance, and the organizational environment.

Another valuable feature is the numerous examples of methods of using action research in the school environment. Real-life situations are presented that contain actual vignettes with practical solutions that any educator can utilize in improving education. This unique feature has been appreciated by teachers during in-service teacher training in giving specific examples of where education research can be used in the classroom. These examples can help to stimulate the thinking of teachers and administrators so that they can make improvements within their own classroom and school.

Several other features of this book include:

- A procedure for using action research in the school environment.
- A model of action research with examples.
- A comprehensive description of how action research varies from the use of qualitative and quantitative research methodology.
- Examples of benchmarking techniques that can aid an educator in using action research.

- Examples on how to conduct literature reviews.
- A detailed explanation of collecting data and analyzing this data in a practical manner.
- Practical tips and strategies to analyze data using basic statistical methods.
- Samples of teacher action research projects and references.
- How to construct graphs using Microsoft Excel.
- Methods of evaluating action research.
- Explanation of how to conduct a formal action research proposal.
- Strategies in conducting interviews and surveys.

The technique of action research, as presented in this book, has been applied in schools and taught for several years. For example, this technique has been used in major school districts to improve performance on test scores, teacher morale, quality of student learning, leadership, discipline, and safety. The principles of action research have also been implemented as a process to diagnose school organizational problems and to develop specific action plans to help improve the overall performance of schools, colleges, and universities. Several schools have implemented the principles from this book. Professionals have used this research to study student discipline problems and absenteeism, student motivation and self-esteem, teacher morale and stress, and overall student performance in the classroom.

This book contains a rich source of educational and reference aids so that educators can apply the principles of action research. Some of these aids include:

- A sample of educational problems.
- A sample of field-based educational issues.
- Detailed listing of references and benchmarking techniques.
- Samples of teacher action research projects.
- Examples of using action research to improve the overall school management.
- Case illustrations and figures in understanding action research.
- Seventy-five ideas for conducing action research.
- Actual examples of surveys and questionnaires used in action research.

ORGANIZATION OF THE BOOK

This book has been written for an educator to understand the basics of action research and to apply action research in solving school problems and making improvements. Each chapter builds upon the other. Given that much of the material in this book has been developed and refined throughout the years through teaching the subject at the graduate level and in educator in-service workshops, the information is practical and straightforward.

ACKNOWLEDGMENTS

The author acknowledges the many people who have contributed by providing support and input for the preparation of this book. Special appreciation is given to the author's students, colleagues, former business associates, and to Susan Webb for typing the manuscript. Appreciation is especially extended to the many school districts where the author has worked or given seminars, such as Chicago Public Schools, Bellwood School District 88, Cicero School District 99, Lake Central School Corporation, Proviso Township High Schools, West Chicago District 33, Michigan City Township High Schools, Findlay Schools, Concordia University, and Lutheran Church Missouri Synod Schools. Last, the author would like to extend his gratitude to his family: his wife, Annette; children, Jonathan, Stephanie, and Justin; his mother, Estelle; and late father, Raymond.

THE NATURE OF
EDUCATIONAL RESEARCH

PRINCIPLES OF RESEARCH

A working definition of research is the systematic process of attempting to find a solution to a problem (when the solution is not known) using an acceptable methodology. The argument can be made that if the solution to the problem is known, then a person merely needs to find the solution, and, therefore, systematic research is not necessary. Research involves more than just finding a known solution to a problem. It entails a careful undertaking to discover new facts and relationships concerning a solution that is unknown.

Many people use the term *research* loosely, when, in fact, the process of research is much more investigative and scientific. As early as the 1930s, the famous philosopher John Dewey (1933) outlined the scientific process of research consisting of: problem identification, developing a hypothesis (or educated guess), collecting and analyzing data, and drawing conclusions concerning the data and hypothesis (see Figure 1.1).

The basis of Dewey's description of scientific research is somewhat similar to the process used today. Although variations in the process exist, depending upon the research methodology, this process is generally accepted as a general framework for scientific inquiry. Several common

Problem Identification

➡ Clarification of main question
➡ Description of hypothesis
➡ Collection and analysis of data
➡ Drawing conclusions
➡ Rejecting or accepting hypothesis

Figure 1.1. John Dewey's Scientific Process of Research

terms are used in research. The term *theory* can be described as "an explanation of observed phenomena." For example, most educators have learned Abraham Maslow's Sociological Human Needs Theory. Maslow (1943) attempted to describe the sociological needs of human beings through a hierarchy of lower-level and higher-level human needs. In essence, his explanation is called a research thesis. Piaget's Theory of Human Development is another example of a theory (1926). Many of Piaget's theories are familiar to educators who attempt to understand the development of children. Theories are an important part of research because the result of research often concludes with the development of a theory.

Another term that is used in research is called the *variable*. A variable is a quantitative way to describe a concept. Typically, the two kinds of variables are *independent variables* and *dependent variables*. Independent variables are defined as the cause of some action and dependent variables refer to the effect of some action. For example, if we were to reconstruct an experimental research study based on the question of whether fluoride reduces tooth decay, we might have two variables. The first variable, fluoride toothpaste, would be the independent variable (i.e., the effect of the fluoride on tooth decay), and the second variable, the dependent variable, could be the difference in the tooth decay (i.e., the reduction of tooth decay). Variables are often used in research to help describe a cause-and-effect relationship.

One of the more popular terms used in research is the *hypothesis*. A hypothesis can be described as simply an "educated guess." A more scientific definition of a hypothesis might be "the description of the relationship among two variables." Researchers often use two types of hypotheses: the *null hypothesis* and the *directional hypothesis*. The null hypothesis states that there is no difference or relationship between two variables. For example, a null hypothesis might state that, "there will be no difference between the use of fluoride and the reduction of tooth decay." An example of a directional hypothesis is when the researcher makes a guess that there will be a difference in two variables, such as, "the use of fluoride toothpaste will reduce tooth decay." Although both null and directional hypotheses are used in research, the null hypothesis is probably more popular because it tends to prevent the researcher from having a bias.

QUANTITATIVE VERSUS QUALITATIVE RESEARCH

Given that research is the scientific approach to solve a problem when the answer is not known, a researcher can undertake different approaches in this endeavor. The process of seeking truth is defined as *epistemology*. This philosophy of science describes how researchers acquire knowledge. Basically, the two methods of epistemology are called *quantitative* and *qualitative*. Quantitative research is a type of scientific inquiry that is very objective in which the researcher attempts to be detached from the actual subjects of the study. Quantitative researchers are characteristic of the classical medical scientists who study and independently make observations about the cause and effect of variables. Qualitative researchers, on the other hand, are much more personally involved with their study. Qualitative research is more naturalistic, emergent, and case oriented. A typical qualitative researcher might be a person who actually goes into the natural setting and makes observations. For example, if a researcher is studying the behavior of monkeys, the qualitative researcher might go into the natural environment of monkeys and become part of their everyday life and make narrative observations. Figure 1.2 shows a description of these two types of epistemology research methods.

Different methods of research can be categorized as being more quantitative than qualitative (see Figure 1.3). Four popular types of quantitative research are: experimental, casual comparative, correlational, and descriptive. *Experimental* research is concerned with the cause and effect of variables. The purpose of correlational research is to determine the relationship of variables, which can also be used for

Quantitative	Qualitative
▸ Uses numerical data to describe phenomena	▸ Studies the natural setting of the subject
▸ Assumes objective reality	▸ Assumes researcher is involved in the study to some extent
▸ Constructs a hypothesis and uses variables	▸ Assumes each study is independent to itself and emergent
▸ Studies behavior in natural or contrived settings	▸ Studies theories and concepts that are often derived during the research
▸ Uses statistical analysis to analyze data and make conclusions	▸ A hypothesis is not always made, but may include a tentative hypothesis
▸ Accepts or rejects a hypothesis	▸ Makes narrative descriptions in making conclusions

Figure 1.2.   Characteristics of Quantitative and Qualitative Research

prediction. *Causal comparative* research is very similar to experimental research, but it is research that is conducted after the data has been collected (expost facto). An example would be the study of the cause and effect of cigarette smoking and cancer after people have died. *Descriptive* (survey) *research* is research that attempts to describe the present status of phenomena, such as administering a survey to acquire people's feelings about the school environment.

Four popular types of qualitative research are: historical, ethnography, phenomelogical and cultural, and the case study. *Historical research* is concerned with answering questions regarding the past, such as conducting an autobiography. *Ethnography* generally describes people within social environments. *Phenomelogical and cultural research* tends to study various phenomena and cultures of people within an environment. *Case studies* generally are used to study deviant group or information-rich subjects, such as gifted students, in their natural setting.

Quantitative	Qualitative
▸ Experimental	▸ Historical
▸ Causal comparative	▸ Ethnography
▸ Correlational	▸ Phenomenology and cultural
▸ Descriptive or survey	▸ Case studies

Figure 1.3.   Types of Quantitative and Qualitative Research

Quantitative
➡ A scientific approach to undertaking research

Qualitative
➡ A naturalistic and emergent approach to enquiry

Action Research
➡ A process of solving problems and making improvements

Figure 1.4.   Three Approaches to Research

ACTION RESEARCH PRINCIPLES

Simply stated, action research is a systematic process of solving educational problems and making improvements. Action research is different from quantitative and qualitative research, but has characteristics of both. An action researcher utilizes an appropriate intervention to collect and analyze data and to implement actions to address educational issues. Action research is suitable for educators as a practical process because it does not require elaborate statistical analysis (e.g., quantitative research), or lengthy narrative explanations (e.g., qualitative research), but is more concerned with solving a problem in an efficient and feasible manner (Figure 1.4). Also, while traditional research methods have given much more concern for relating the findings to other settings or populations, action research is more concerned with improvements within the context of the study (i.e., solving a given problem). Figure 1.4 describes these three approaches to research (Tomal, 1996).

2

ACTION RESEARCH

HISTORY OF ACTION RESEARCH

Although traces of action research theory can be found in the writings of such philosophers as Galileo, Aristotle, and Newton, one of the earliest philosophers to contribute a foundation for action research in education was John Dewey (*How We Think,* 1933). Dewey, an American, developed a progressive and scientific method of problem solving. Dewey's practical model of scientific inquiry, previously presented in chapter 1 (Figure 1.1), was viewed as being revolutionary during his time. Dewey viewed the classroom as a democratic community and felt that educators should be skeptical of teaching and should be concerned with reflection and improvement. Dewey's steps to educational research are similar to quantitative research methodology, although he emphasized more practicality than basic scientific research.

Many researchers have credited the actual cornerstone of action research to Kurt Lewin (French & Raven, 1995; Tomal, 1997; and Lippitt, 1958). Lewin, a prolific theorist and practitioner, founded the Research Center for Group Dynamics at the Massachusetts Institute of Technology, where group dynamics and action research models and theories were developed. Lewin applied action research strategies as a methodology in behavioral science in attempting to solve sociological problems. He felt that action research programs were crucial in addressing social change issues and making social improvements. Lewin emphasized the need for collaboration and group inquiry in collecting information about social issues and developing action plans to solve these social problems (Lewin, 1947). Lewin's methods did not gain widespread popularity in the business and educational fields until the 1970s, when management consultants began using the principles of action research to improve organizational effectiveness. Although the use of action research flourished in the business world during the 1980s, it has only been within the last decade that action research has been widely used and formally applied in the educational environment (French & Bell, 1995; Sagor, 1992).

In action research, the researcher is concerned with using a systematic process in solving educational problems and making improvements. The researcher utilizes appropriate interventions to collect and analyze data and then to implement actions to address educational issues. Action research is suitable for educators as a practical process because it generally does not require elaborate statistical analysis. Also, although traditional research methods have shown much concern for generalizability (i.e., applicability of the findings to other settings or populations), action research is more concerned with improvement within the context of the study. Richard Sagor (1992), in his book *How to Conduct Collaborative Action Research*, emphasizes this point by stating: "As action researchers, you don't need to worry about the generalizability of your data because you are not seeking to define the ultimate truth of learning theory. Your goal is to understand what is happening in your school or classroom and to determine what might improve things in that context" (Sagor, p. 8).

Several features of action research distinguish it from other research methods. In traditional research, the researcher usually develops a null hypothesis as an objective basis to undertake a study. The researcher then sets out to either accept or reject this hypothesis. Scientific conclusions are later drawn. Action research does not entail creating a null hypothesis but rather focuses on defining a problem, collecting data, and taking action to solve the problem. Also, the action researcher is less concerned with statistical analysis as compared to the quantitative researcher.

Action research is also different from qualitative research. Qualitative researchers are generally concerned about discovering information about data-rich cases found in natural settings and then making inductive conclusions. Action research is much more direct in its purpose. Since the goal is to solve a given problem and make improvements, action researchers rely less on scientific inquiry and inductive reasoning, and more on the practicality and feasibility of solving a given issue.

Another feature of action research is the collaborative nature of the work. Generally, action research is conducted by a change agent (i.e., consultant, researcher, educator, or administrator) who works with identified subjects within the context of a group (classroom, school, or organization) in conducting the study. The change agent acts as a catalyst in collecting data and then working with the group in a collaborative effort to develop actions to address the issues. Action research is often considered a process as much as a research methodology. This process is concerned with the systematic collecting of data, which is analyzed and fed back to the subjects so that action plans can be systematically developed. Therefore, action research is distinguished from other research methodologies because of the collaborative effort of the researcher in working with the subjects and developing action plans to make improvements (Tomal, 1996).

Before educators began using action research methodology on a widespread basis, action research was utilized within the business world by organization development consultants. Organizational consultants (OD practitioners) have used action research principles to make operational and performance improvements within organizations (French & Bell, 1995). OD practitioners have been generally concerned with improving employee morale, productivity, profitability, teamwork, communication, and quality of work life.

A final distinguishing feature of action research is the researcher's use of various interventions (i.e., set of structured activities), which provide the mechanism for the research action. These interventions include such techniques as team building, survey feedback, problem-solving strategies, intergroup activities, diagnostic assessments, interviews, role negotiations, conflict resolutions, third-party peace making, visioning, socio-technical systems, statistical process controls, strategic planning, and a host of other creative schemes. Understanding just a few of these interventions can allow an educator to undertake worthwhile research. Figure 2.1 illustrates some of the typical interventions used by OD consultants for various organizational problems.

Problem/Issue: **Organizational inefficiency and poor leadership**
➡*Intervention*
   Survey feedback
   Total quality management
   Visioning
   Cultural study
   Socio-technical system
   Leadership grid
Problem/Issue: **Poor morale and teamwork**
➡*Intervention*
   Team building
   Conflict resolution
   Quality of work life
Problem/Issue: **Group and organizational conflict**
➡*Intervention*
   Peacemaking
   Conflict resolution
   Team building
   Role negotiating
   Sensitivity training
Problem/Issue: **Career and performance difficulties**
➡*Intervention*
   Team building
   Coaching
   Education

Figure 2.1. Organizational Issues and Possible Intervention Method

Much like the OD practitioner, administrators can utilize the same interventions in addressing a multitude of educational issues. Likewise, action research is useful for teachers as a practical and sensible methodology for making classroom improvements.

ACTION RESEARCH MODEL

Kurt Lewin was an initial pioneer in establishing the action research model, but many researchers have proposed variations of his model (Beckhard, 1969; Argyris, 1970; Shepard, 1960; French & Bell, 1995). Although variations on this model exist, depending upon the nature of the researcher's discipline, the general framework is similar to Lewin's original model. For example, a general model of action research derived from the work of Kurt Lewin is illustrated in Figure 2.2. The use of this model would be essentially the same whether an administrator desires to improve staff morale, a teacher seeks to improve classroom discipline, or a dean desires to improve student attendance.

The process of action research is very similar to the approach used by a physician in treating a patient. The doctor first makes an initial problem statement based upon the patient's complaint (e.g., patient's back hurts), conducts a series of medical diagnostic tests (data collection), discusses the results of these tests with the patient (analysis and feedback), makes a decision and treats the patient (planning and taking action), and then follows up on the patient's condition (evaluation and follow up).

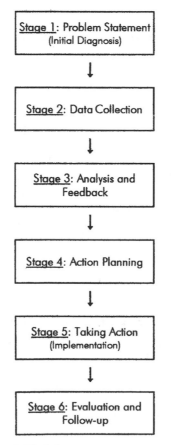

Figure 2.2. Action Research Model

Let's explore an example of applying this action research model for an educational issue, such as staff development. We will start with the assumption that the school principal does not know which of the teacher developmental areas are in need of improvement. Also, we will assume that the principal would like the teachers to develop a feeling of ownership (i.e., "buy in") to the process rather than feeling as if the proposed developmental effect is being mandated. Figure 2.3 lists typical examples of professional development needs.

Stage 1: Problem Statement (Initial Diagnosis)

The process begins with the principal identifying the initial problem based upon a "felt need" that her faculty would benefit from continuing professional development. Her initial diagnosis suggests a need for teacher skill development, based upon requests from the faculty, reading research articles, and the observation of teacher and student per-

Student-Centered Issues

- ▶ Building self-esteem
- ▶ Improving study habits
- ▶ Improving student character
- ▶ Developing student interpersonal relationships
- ▶ Helping students work together
- ▶ Helping students deal with change
- ▶ Improving student motivation

School-Centered Issues

- ▶ Dealing with financial constraints
- ▶ Gaining more parent involvement
- ▶ Improving the organizational structure
- ▶ Improving leadership
- ▶ Developing better teamwork
- ▶ Developing school improvement plan

Teacher-Classroom Issues

- ▶ Improving student attendance
- ▶ Managing student conflict
- ▶ Counseling students
- ▶ Helping students manage strong emotions
- ▶ Teaching challenging students
- ▶ Handling disciplinary problems
- ▶ Handling student complaints

Instructional-Development Issues

- ▶ Improving test scores
- ▶ Improving instructional techniques
- ▶ Developing team teaching
- ▶ Enhancing instruction
- ▶ Improving curriculum
- ▶ Improving student achievement

Figure 2.3. Examples of Professional Development Needs

formance. The principal might explore different methods to collect data (e.g., survey, needs assessment) for determining skill deficiencies or areas in need of improvement for the faculty. She would also conduct preliminary costs, time estimates, possible facilitators, tentative workshop dates, and other logistics prior to initiating and announcing her intentions. It is important during this initial diagnosis stage that the principal conduct a reasonable amount of planning in order to decide whether to undertake the action research project.

Stage 2: Data Collection

Data collection, the second stage, can be accomplished by several methods, such as: needs assessment, interviews, and group meetings. For example, if the principal elects to administer a needs assessment, this approach can be useful in ensuring confidentiality and anonymity. A typical needs assessment might consist of a list of professional development topics (e.g., class management, learning styles, curriculum development, stress management, counseling students, and instructional techniques), where the respondents are asked to assign a value to each topic (i.e., Likert Grading Scale) indicating the degree of need for further development.

Random one-on-one follow-up interviews with teachers could also be conducted to gain clarification about the topics identified in the needs assessment period. This information could be helpful in gaining additional information concerning additional organizational issues and isolating specific development needs for the teachers.

Stage 3: Analysis and Feedback

In this stage, the results of the survey could be made by calculating simple mean averages, then ranking the professional development topics in order of importance. The principal could then conduct a feedback session with the faculty to review the rankings, gain clarification about the results, and obtain input from them regarding the desired topics. Although preliminary action planning might occur in this feedback session, the primary objective is to gain clarification about the collected data. Also, as a practical matter, various organizational issues (e.g., time constraints, teacher schedules, and need for further analysis) could hinder the principal from making final actions or commitments without conducting the feedback session.

The feedback session is a crucial stage in an action research process that provides an element of collaboration. This stage also helps develop communications, trust, and mutual support between the principal and faculty. The first three stages of the action research model (problem statement, data collection, and analysis and feedback) can be described as the problem-solving segment of the action research process. These stages serve to identify the cause(s) of the problem and specific areas in need of improvement.

Stage 4: Action Planning

Stage 4, action planning, is the decision-making segment of the process. It involves deciding upon a course of action to address the issue(s). This process can be accomplished through a number of methods. The principal may make in-service training plans (i.e., final selection of topics, scheduling and program logistics). A faculty involvement team, consisting of selected teachers, could also be assembled to develop and implement the action plans. Prior to implementing the actions, the final plan could also be reviewed by the entire faculty.

Stage 5: Taking Action (Implementation)

In stage 5, the action plan would be implemented (i.e., in-service program). To reinforce a collaborative process, the principal might want to actually participate in the in-service program. This implementation stage represents the actual action part of the action research process. At the conclusion of the workshop, an evaluation could also be conducted.

Stage 6: Evaluation and Follow Up

A formal assessment should be conducted in the final stage (evaluation and follow up). This stage entails following up and assessing the results of the action. Action research, unlike other methods, includes implementation and evaluation as part of the process. For example, the principal might administer a workshop evaluation, conduct follow-up surveys, or measure actual benefits from in-service programs through student achievements, performance observations, etc. This stage could also act as a vehicle for continuous improvement for the organization.

Let's explore another example of applying the action research model, such as improving classroom discipline. We'll start with the assumption that a teacher is experiencing a high number of student disruptions and disciplinary incidents in her classroom.

STATEMENT OF THE PROBLEM (INITIAL DIAGNOSIS)

The teacher recognizes that she is experiencing a high number of disciplinary problems and would like to make improvements. In this first step, she would start with an initial analysis of the disciplinary situation. The teacher examines the overall dynamics of the classroom, such as the types of disciplinary offenses, when the offenses are being committed, who is primarily committing the offenses, and the teacher investigates the current disciplinary policies and procedures. This step can be called *situational analysis*. An analogy can be made to a medical doctor who first examines the patient and completes a history and physical report. The doctor records the patient's symptoms, past and present health problems, and medications being taken. Likewise, the teacher should collect all the relevant information in order to make an accurate diagnosis.

Stage 2: Data Collection

In the second stage, the teacher begins by investigating the facts (i.e., data collection) surrounding the disciplinary problems. The teacher should examine the "who, what, where, and when." The teacher should note any deviations from what has normally been experienced in the past. For example, the teacher might identify increased incidents of verbal fighting and harassment among students than experienced before. The teacher should also identify the "what is" versus "what is not." For example, the "what is" could be identified as dominantly younger students (freshman and sophomores) who are harassing each other versus junior and senior students (the "what is not"). In this manner the teacher is able to dissect the problem by pinpointing the exact facts of the disciplinary situation.

Stage 3: Analysis and Feedback

After the teacher collects information regarding the types and nature of disciplinary offenses, she is ready for the analysis stage. In this stage, she should actually complete a problem-solving phase of this process by identifying the most likely causes for disciplinary problems. If there is more than one cause, she could rank them in order of importance. The teacher might also want to discuss the nature of the disciplinary offences with her students. By discussing the disciplinary problems with the students, she might gain more insight regarding other causes of the problem.

Stage 4: Action Planning

The action planning stage is similar to a decision-making process. After the teacher identifies the types of disciplinary problems, she should begin listing various solutions to resolve the disciplinary issues. Some solutions might consist of: separating problem students from one another, making curriculum or instructional changes, and changing the classroom rules and policies. The action-planning phase concludes with identifying the most likely solution(s) for resolving the disciplinary incidents. This stage might also include analysis of each action. The merits of each action should be examined for their strengths and weaknesses in resolving disciplinary problems. For example, if the disciplinary problem tends to be an increase in student assaults, the teacher could work with a committee to examine possible solutions, such as educating students about assaults, making improvements within the classroom environment, removing a problem student from the classroom, or building the self-esteem of students.

Stage 5: Taking Action

Although this stage entails that the teacher actually incorporates the action(s), the teacher might also want to develop a contingency plan. A contingency plan involves developing an alternative course of action should the initial action prove unsuccessful. For example, if the problem is student assaults, the contingency plan might include harsher penalties for offenders, more elaborate classroom changes, or increased security.

Stage 6: Evaluation and Follow up

The final stage involves evaluating the results of the action(s). After implementing the solution the teacher needs to evaluate the results. Once an evaluation has been made, continuous improvement processes could also be incorporated.

DEVELOPING AN ACTION RESEARCH PROPOSAL

The development of a formal action research study (e.g., thesis, dissertation, funded study, and comprehensive school study) requires careful planning and execution. Before undertaking a formal study, a research proposal should first be developed. The proposal serves as a plan in guiding the educator through the research process. There are five basic steps in preparing the proposal (Figure 2.4).

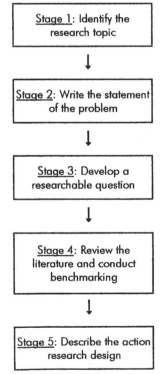

Figure 2.4.   Developing an Action Research Proposal

The process beings by identifying the topic, such as student motivation. Step two involves writing the statement of the problem. For example, an educator might first begin with an issue, such as "students are not reading at home during their leisure time." The teacher then begins to formulate an action research question (step three), such as "I wonder if there are things I can do to help motivate the students to read during their leisure time?" or "I wonder if extrinsic rewards, such as gift certificates or prizes, would help motivate students to read?" The fourth step in preparing the research proposal entails reviewing the literature. In this stage, the teacher could read several articles from journals, magazines, books, and other resource materials and identify possible methods to provide incentives for students. The final step of the preparation plan involves the teacher thinking about how he or she might conduct the design of the study. The design entails the process of collecting data, analyzing the data, and developing action plans and evaluation.

Although many educators do not need to develop an entire proposal in order to conduct an action research study, when this is necessary a formal proposal would contain similar components of a quantitative or qualitative study (Figure 2.5).

Although variations exist in the actual components of a formal action research study, like any research study, Figure 2.5 represents the general framework. The proposal is similar to a complete study, except that the study would contain actual data, analysis of the data, and the findings. Also, both the proposal and study should contain an abstract that represents a one-page executive review of the entire proposal or study.

Chapter one of the proposal should begin with a subtitle called *The Nature of the Problem*. The purpose of this section is to set the stage for the topic. Begin by writing about the topic in a general fashion with supporting sources and references. The researcher writes about the topic from a broad perspective and then narrows the scope of the writing to specifically address the researcher's own problem. Action research, unlike quantitative research studies, does not contain a hypothesis. The statement of the problem is substituted for the hypothesis. The statement of problem is, in general, a rather brief paragraph indicating precisely the problem being confronted. It represents a succinct description of the issue.

Most proposals contain a section called *Definition of Terms*, which gives descriptions of the main terms and how they are defined in the

Abstract
Table of Contents
Chapter 1: Introduction
  Nature of the problem
  Statement of the problem
  Purpose of the study
  Definition of terms
  Significance of the study
  Organization of the study
Chapter 2: Review of Literature
  (Benchmarking)
Chapter 3: Action Research Design
  Subjects
  Procedures
  Data collection
  Instrumentation
  Proposed action
Chapter 4: Analysis of Data
  Proposed presentation of data
  Proposed analysis of data
Chapter 5: Proposed Evaluation
  Procedure of evaluating results
  Conclusions
  Proposed recommendations
References
Appendix

Figure 2.5. Contents of an Action Research Proposal

study. An action research study might also contain a subtitle called *Significance of the Study*. Researchers should explain why this problem is significant and the reasons why making improvements can be helpful. Another subtitle that is often used in research is called *Limitations*. Limitations are those factors that hinder the study from being ideal. Action research generally does not need to describe limitations of the study although limitations could be identified. Examples of limitations might be: a lack of random sampling of subjects, a lack of statistical analysis using tests of significance, and the lack of systematic data collection in a controlled setting.

The *Review of Literature* (chapter two) is an important part of the study because it represents the body of knowledge relating to the topic.

This helps the researcher in learning about other studies that have been completed regarding the topic and their results. The researcher can obtain many useful ideas through conducting a review of the literature.

This literature search generally includes an extensive review of dissertations, professional publications, journal articles, books, publications, and sometimes personal interviews with expert people. Although the review of literature is common to qualitative and quantitative research, it is less important to action research. In action research, which could include review of past publications, benchmarking, and a technique of discovering the best practices of other people and institutions, is often more valuable.

Chapter three of the action research proposal consists of the *intervention* to be used to collect data. The idea of collecting data involves selecting the best intervention method to obtain the most useful information. The array of interventions has significantly increased over the years largely because of organization development consultants. Consultants have utilized a number of interventions in making organizational improvements. Some of the more popular action research interventions used by educators are the survey, group process, interview, observation, and assessment of school records, student grades, etc. A more detailed description of these interventions is addressed in chapter 4.

Chapter four of the action research proposal is the *analysis of data*. In this section, the educator describes the method used to analyze the data. The researcher might use basic statistics and inductive reasoning in making the analysis. The use of statistics and data analysis is covered in more detail in chapter 5. The last chapter is called the *Proposed Evaluation*. Here, the researcher provides a brief, tentative explanation of how the results of the study will be evaluated. Depending upon the nature of the topic, this section would vary in scope and length.

BENCHMARKING

The strategy of *benchmarking*, which can be used as the literature search, is an outgrowth of the total quality movement and is a process of identifying the best practices of other schools and adapting these practices as a basis for solving problems and making educational improvements. Benchmarking is similar to a literature review, except that it is less concerned with identifying academic and scholarly research publications and more concerned with identifying best practices. Establishing standards based upon nationwide school practices can be a crucial component in making educational improvements. *Dantotsu,* a Japanese term, means "striving to be the best of the best," which is the essence of the benchmarking philosophy (Camp, 1989).

The benchmarking process was first used by the Japanese to seek out the best practices of their competitors and adapt them for their own use. The notion is to obtain superiority by practicing what the best companies are doing and continuously striving to make quality improvements. Therefore, the ultimate goal of benchmarking in action research is to utilize this process to identify actions that can be used to solve the problem and make improvements. Benchmarking is similar to a literature review, except that it centers on identifying practical educational practices rather than published scholarly work because the nature of action research is to solve the problem. However, when appropriate, a combination of benchmarking and literature review can be used in the action research process if the researcher believes that both are needed to address the issue (Tomal, 1998).

Several methods can be used in the benchmarking process (Figure 2.6). For example, if the goal is to improve student reading, the researcher could utilize methods such as visiting other school reading programs, contacting outside universities and vendors, consulting reading experts, attending professional association conferences, and reviewing magazines and journals on the subject of reading. The researcher might also assemble a team of fellow educators in which each of them could benchmark a different area. This teamwork would allow the benchmarking to be conducted more efficiently. The members could later pool their findings together for group discussion. The team could also collaborate in selecting the best method(s) to address the topic of reading. Although benchmarking can be a valuable method, the process requires a commitment of time and human resources and the researcher needs to be willing to make this investment.

External Educational Source
→ Other school districts
→ Schools within the district
→ Colleges and universities
→ Libraries and resource centers

Internal Education Sources
→ Departments within the school
→ Experts within the school
→ School library and Internet

Informational Resources
→ Articles and journals
→ Government agencies
→ Professional organizations
→ Seminars and workshops
→ Commercial products

Outside Professionals
→ Professional consultants
→ Educational vendors

Other Contacts
→ Parents and community
→ Local school board members
→ Business and government

Figure 2.6.   Methods of Benchmarking in Action Research

ETHICAL AND LEGAL CONSIDERATIONS

Researchers, regardless of the type of research they are conducting, should always be concerned with protecting their subjects and avoiding legal problems. Nothing is worse in research than to have harm come to a subject and the researcher become faced with a legal suit. Most institutions (e.g., colleges and universities) have a research committee on human subjects, which is a body of internal professionals who reviews and approves any research prior to the start of the research study. This committee is charged with ensuring that the proposed research conforms with institutional and professional standards in conducting research. Several professional organizations (American Psychological Association and American Educational Research Association) have provided guidelines on research ethics and protocol (see appendix A).

Some of the ethical standards outlined by the American Psychological Association (APA) include: obtaining an informed consent from the subjects, avoiding excessive financial inducements for participation, minimizing invasiveness (collection of information that could cause misconceptions or excessive risk to the subjects), ensuring that participation in the study is voluntary, agreeing to share information with the participants, agreeing not to deceive the participants, protecting the subjects from harm (physical, emotional, and mental), and taking reasonable measures to honor all commitments that have been made to the participants (APA, 1992).

3

DATA COLLECTION METHODS

THE NATURE OF DATA COLLECTION

There are many methods to collect data in action research. Selecting the best method is a crucial aspect to ensure the acquisition of relevant and valid information. The old expression, "garbage in, garbage out" applies to action research because if you fail to use the appropriate method of collecting data, your research will be compromised. In planning to collect data, the researcher also needs to consider the type of analysis of the data to be performed. A common mistake of educators is to select a method of collecting data without planning for the best method of analysis. For example, if a researcher is planning to collect data through the use of a questionnaire, he or she needs to plan how the actual responses to each of the items will be analyzed. A pilot testing of the questionnaire and analysis of the data should be performed. This will allow the researcher to identify more appropriate methods of collecting data or the need to revise the design of the questionnaire so that it is more suitable for analysis. For example, the researcher might decide, after piloting the questionnaire, that a different type of scale is needed in order to complete a comprehensive analysis. It is best to identify these problems during the pilot phase rather than waiting until all the data has been collected. When planning for data collection, some basic questions of who, what, where, when, and how should be addressed.

Who are the subjects of the study? Researchers should start with a clear understanding of the characteristics of the subjects of the study. For example, if the researcher is concerned with improving the reading ability of fourth grade students, then the method of data collection might be different, depending upon the number of students and grade levels at the school. If there are only a small number of students, then a selection of interviewing students might be more appropriate than conducting a questionnaire, which might be more appropriate for a large number of students. Also, the questionnaire might be useless if administered to a group of students who can't read. For example, if there is only one class consisting of 20 students, then the researchers may interview the teacher to gain information about the students' reading ability. Also, the decision whether to include the entire class in the study or to consider dividing the class in half and using two different types of methods need to be considered. The type of data collection used could vary, depending upon the desired outcomes.

What data needs to be collected? The action researcher needs to take a strategic approach to determine what data to collect. Collecting unneeded data or the wrong kind of information can limit the study. For example, if there is concern with the reading ability of sixth grade students, the researcher needs to decide whether to collect reading scores from the class, homework assignments, assessments from parents, or standardized tests. Also, the researcher might need to collect data that can be later assessed to determine if actions to improve reading have helped. If the researcher cannot collect the same type of information, then the study will be compromised.

Where is the data? There are two types of data in conducting an action research study. One is the *raw data* that will be collected and assessed in order to define the actual cause of a problem, which is the basis on which action plans can be developed. For example, this data could be the information collected from administering a survey to students regarding their study habits. The second type of data, called *benchmarked data,* is related information that is often collected in order to provide possible solutions for developing the action plans and making improvements. For example, if the data to be collected concerns the reading ability of students, then the researcher must also be able to benchmark and collect information regarding different viable reading curriculum, instruction, or intervention methods that could be used to improve the reading abilities of the students (i.e., benchmarked data). Assessing this type of information can help the researcher in deciding whether to conduct the action research and how much time and resources will potentially be needed. Moreover, the researcher might also plan to collect benchmarking information on reading while, at the same time, collecting the raw data collection from the subjects. This process could help the researcher be more efficient in the action research process.

When will the data be obtained? Just as important as collecting the right type of data is the researcher's ability to collect data at the appropriate time. For example, the data might best be collected during the beginning of the school year versus at a time when the students have more distractions, such as close to a holiday, scheduled activity, or end of the school year.

How will the data be collected? The researcher needs to be concerned with how the data is collected and whether consent forms or other confidentiality agreements should be used. Likewise, the researcher should be concerned with the method of collecting data so that it does not harm the students in any way psychologically or emotionally. Also, care should be taken to secure the data so that the information does not have a negative effect upon the learning environment. Although numerous methods can be used to collect data in research, some of the more common methods used in action research are listed in Figure 3.1.

OBSERVING

Observing is one of the more popular methods of data collection for all research studies. The many techniques of observing range from structured observations using tally sheets to an open, unstructured approach. Whether the researcher uses a structured or open process, skill is needed.

Observing

→ Direct observation
→ Anecdotal notes
→ Check lists
→ Journals

Surveying

→ Group surveys
→ Individual surveys
→ Two-way surveys
→ One-way surveys

Interviewing

→ Group interviews
→ Focus groups
→ Individual interviews
→ Structured interviews

Assessing

→ Portfolios
→ Testing
→ Records
→ Recordings

Figure 3.1. Methods of Data Collection

Direct Observations

One of the advantages to using direct observation is the researcher's ability to obtain actual firsthand information regarding subjects. Direct observation can give the researcher the opportunity to collect data in a real-life situation that cannot be obtained through secondary information, such as self reports and assessments. The researcher can also obtain information that is more reliable than relying upon data obtained from the subjects themselves or third-party individuals. However, there are some limitations. It is possible that if subjects know they are being observed, their pattern of behavior could be altered. For example, if a principal decides to observe a classroom, undoubtedly the performance of the students and teacher will increase. This concept is sometimes called the *Hawthorne Effect*. This concept suggests that the mere giving of attention to people will cause their performance to increase. Various techniques can be used to reduce the Hawthorne Effect, such as use of one-way mirrors or simply positioning oneself in the least conspicuous manner in the room (Mayo, 1939).

The observational technique can be more time consuming that using other data collection methods. If a larger number of subjects need to be observed, then other methods, such as interviews, questionnaires, and assessments might be more practical. However, even with the limitations, the advantages of the observational method can produce superior results for the researcher.

Whether an observer uses a structured or unstructured approach, the researcher should be aware of factors that hinder the observer in making accurate recordings (Frick & Semmel, 1978). Figure 3.2 lists some of the factors that hinder observations.

Observers must continually refine their skills to guard against these factors. One common problem for observers is the tendency to "see

Factor: Halo Effect
➡ *Definition:* Tendency to always view subjects positively or negatively

Factor: Leniency Effect
➡ *Definition:* Tendency to give high observational ratings to all subjects—even when differences exist

Factor: Recency Effect
➡ *Definition:* Tendency to give more emphasis to recent behaviors during the observational period

Factor: Central Tendency
➡ *Definition:* Reluctance to rate subjects either high or low and give average ratings

Factor: Rater Indecisiveness
➡ *Definition:* Inability to make categorical judgments about the subjects

Factor: Personal Bias
➡ *Definition:* Tendency to rate subjects based upon the observer's own prejudice

Factor: Contamination
➡ *Definition:* Any conditions that alter the natural setting of the subject's performance, which is being observed

Factor: Observer Omission
➡ *Definition:* Inability of the observer to record all necessary subject behaviors

Factor: Observer Drift
➡ *Definition:* Tendency for observers to lose their concentration and fail to record information

Factor: Intra-observer Reliability
➡ *Definition:* Failure of the observer to consistently agree with his or her observational recordings

Figure 3.2.   Factors that Hinder Observation

Factor: Inter-observer Reliability
➡ *Definition:* Failure of the observer to agree with other observers in collecting data

Factor: Criterion-Related Observer Reliability
➡ *Definition:* Failure of the observer to record data that is in agreement with an established expert's criteria

Figure 3.2.   Factors that Hinder Observation *(continued)*

what they want to see." This inherent bias hinders the observer from being completely objective. For example, if a researcher is studying the misbehavior of children, and he or she is frustrated with the high number of incidents, there might be a tendency to overrate any potential misbehavior that would not otherwise be considered a discipline problem. Therefore, it is important to establish a criteria in which discipline offenses will be rated, as opposed to making general observations.

Another factor that can influence the effectiveness of observation is the degree in which the observer participates in the study (Figure 3.3). If the researcher decides to become a *complete observer,* then he or she should not be involved in any interaction with the subject and try to remain objective and neutral in the natural environment. For example, if a teacher is studying the play of early childhood students, then he or she should allow the children to play without being noticed. This allows the children to participate in their natural setting without any contamination or influence from the educator (i.e., obtrusive measure).

If the teacher decides to act primarily as a *participant observer,* then he or she needs to be well trained in the activity and disciplined in recording observations without being distracted from participation.

Type of Participant: Complete Observer
➡ *Definition:* A nonparticipant who is detached from the study

Type of Participant: Participant Observer
➡ *Definition:* The researcher interacts with the subjects while making observations

Type of Participant: Partial Participant Observer
➡ *Definition:* Researcher has limited interaction with subjects while making observations

Figure 3.3.   Degrees of Observer Participation

Likewise, the *partial participant observer* needs to record information without becoming personally involved in the study. For example, it was once rumored that a researcher was observing the phenomena of the Billy Graham crusade. The researcher began the study by recording general observations. However, as the researcher continued, he became more and more interested in Dr. Graham's message being delivered, to the extent that at the end of the service the researcher actually walked on stage and became part of the service. This is a vivid example of how a researcher can be so personally involved with the study that he or she no longer can act as an unbiased observer. The term that describes this phenomenon is called *reflexivity*, which can be defined as the researcher overly focusing on him or herself as part of the phenomena and then no longer acting as an unbiased observer.

Anecdotal Notes   The method of collecting data through anecdotal notes is similar to qualitative researchers making field notes. Field notes are a form of direct observation and can easily be transferred into anecdotal impressions. The ideas of collecting field notes is to observe everything and anything. They are called *field notes* because the researcher collects information by observing phenomena in its natural setting, such as a classroom or school. A good example of making field notes is the work of famous qualitative researcher, Jane Goodall. Dr. Goodall studied apes and monkeys in their natural setting. She actually lived within their environment and wrote observations in narrative form as she observed these animals in their natural habitat. The ability to make observations and then reflect on these narrative writings can allow the researcher to make general impressions and inductive conclusions (Bernard, 1994). The many methods of making field notes can be based upon pre-established time intervals, specified events, and crucial incidents. The anecdotal record is one that is particularly useful for educators (Figure 3.4).

The key to making anecdotal notes is to quickly record any factual observations, such as incidents or behaviors that are relevant to the study. This record can be very useful in recording information that can be later reflected upon. Piaget used this method to record his observations when he studied his children's development. Anecdotal notes can be recorded by using sheets of paper, index cards, computer software, or any other methods that allow the action researcher to conveniently

Date	Student Name	Comments
5-5	Stephanie	Appears sleepy, distracted and disinterested with doing work.
5-7	Stephanie	Appears engaged, motivated and in deep concentration with work.
5-9	Stephanie	Continues to be engaged and very helpful to other students in explaining how to perform work. Stephanie made comment that she likes the subject matter and helping people.

Figure 3.4.   Observational Anecdotal Form

record observations and organize the material (Piaget, 1926). An analysis of anecdotal notes can then be performed after the data has been collected (Figure 3.5).

Checklists   The use of checklists is a quantitative way to conduct a structured observation. Checklists can serve as a valuable tool in ensuring that the researcher records timely and accurate observations. For

---

Date: 6-2

Student: Justin

Class: Fourth Grade

Observer: Jonathan

Analysis: Based upon the analysis of Justin's performance and behavior over the past week, my impression is that he is a student who either is totally engaged with the subject matter or is disinterested. Justin seems to be most disinterested when working alone. However, he seems to be highly engaged when allowed to work with other students. He has a strong need to develop a helping role for other students, especially when he is able to explain the material. He appears to be a child who needs to work with other students in a collaborative fashion, especially if he can be the leader. Therefore, my impression is that Justin is best suited for cooperative or collaborative teacher environments as opposed to working alone. This impression is supported by my talking with Justin and asking his preference. His statement, based upon my direct questioning, was, "I like working with other students, and it's fun to act as the teacher in the classroom, too."

Figure 3.5.   Anecdotal Notes and Analysis

example, the researcher might find it difficult to record general observations without a structured set of factors to help provide guidance. Several different methods of recording observations can be used with checklists, such as duration recording, frequency recording, interval recording, and continuous recording (Gall, Borg, & Gall, 1996).

The *duration recording* is a method in which the observer records information during a specific elapsed period of time. For example, the observer might record observations while a student is "on task" or "off task" and is engaged or not engaged in activities. The *frequency recording* technique allows the observer to make a tally mark on the checklist each time he or she observes a pre-specified behavior. The *interval recording* involves the observation of behavior at predetermined intervals, such as every three minutes. The observer records the student's behavior at each three-minute interval. *Continuous recording* involves observing all pre-specified behaviors of a student during the observation interval. Because it is difficult to observe all behavior, the observer must focus on specific incidents or behaviors. Checklists can be especially helpful in keeping track of student descriptions, such as gender, time, age, and conditions (Figure 3.6).

Journals   The use of journals is similar to the method of anecdotal recording. Although there are different types of journals, such as logs and diaries, essentially the researcher is observing the situations (i.e., students in a classroom) and making narrative recordings. A log tends to be a more detailed description of events and incidents, and a diary tends to be more of a personal account of one's feelings and events. Therefore,

Date:_____ Student:_____ Gender:_____
Time:_____

Directions: Please mark a check for each time the following behavior is observed.

Student takes notes:_____ Total:_____
Student asks questions:_____ Total:_____
Student responds:_____ Total:_____
Student looks confused:_____ Total:_____
Student works cooperatively:_____ Total:_____
Student gives answer:_____ Total:_____

Figure 3.6.   Sample of Observational Checklist

a journal can be considered as a method of recording the behaviors, feelings, and incidents of subjects (Figure 3.7).

The use of journals can be very helpful for researchers in observing behavior and making a detailed analysis. However, although the use of journals might require more time than making anecdotal notes, journals allow the researcher to obtain more detailed information.

INTERVIEWING

Conducting interviews can be a powerful technique for an action researcher. Interviewing consists of asking questions to an individual or a group of individuals and obtaining their verbal responses. The respondents generally give their candid opinions, which are then directly recorded or paraphrased by the interviewer. These responses also can be transcribed from audiotape, videotape, computer software, or by

---

Student: *Mary*
Observer:
First Entry: *5-7*
I noticed that Mary is very receptive and is diligent in completing her work. She is very observant and is quick to answer questions and is helpful to her fellow students. She does tend to have more difficulty when completing math. When she experiences difficulty she tends to close up and become more introverted. She is reluctant to ask questions when she has difficulty with the subject matter.

Second Entry: *5-9*
I noticed that Mary is very enthusiastic and talkative as she completes her social studies material. She clearly grasps the material and is very confident.

Third Entry: *5-11*
Again, Mary is experiencing difficulty with mathematics. Her behavior is consistent with becoming more introverted when having a difficult time with subject matter. She tends to not ask questions or seek assistance. Therefore, it appears that I need to pay close attention when Mary experiences difficulty and give her probing questions to support her learning.

Figure 3.7.   Researcher's Journal Log

handwritten notes. Although the interviewer is primarily concerned with getting verbal information from the respondents, valuable observations can be made while observing their behavior during their responses that might not be obtained through the use of questionnaires. The interviewing technique also has the advantage of allowing the interviewer to engage in an in-depth discussion with the respondents, which can often lead to more useful and richer information. Also, the researcher can structure his or her questions based on specific areas of interest that can elicit different types of responses (Figure 3.8).

There are some disadvantages in using the interviewing technique, such as time limitations, potential inaccuracy of interpretations of the participant responses, difficulty in interviewing a large number of people, and that some people might not feel comfortable in participating in the interviewing process. Regardless of whether the interviewer conducts a group or individual session, the basic steps for conducting an interviewing session are the same (Figure 3.9).

The first step in conducting the interview is to *prepare the questions*. The questions should be tailored, based upon the information that the researcher wants to obtain. If the researcher is planning to interview a student regarding his or her difficulties in learning, the questions can be structured based upon feelings, situations, and behaviors that best elicit responses and get to the root of the problem. It also might be important

Individual behaviors

Group behaviors

    ▸ Social dynamics
    ▸ Feelings and emotions
    ▸ Scenarios and situations
    ▸ Environment
    ▸ Processes and organizational issues
    ▸ Change situations
    ▸ Roles and responsibilities
    ▸ Factual events
    ▸ Motives and emotions
    ▸ Triggering events and conditions
    ▸ Objects, places, and time frames

Figure 3.8.   Types of Questioning Techniques

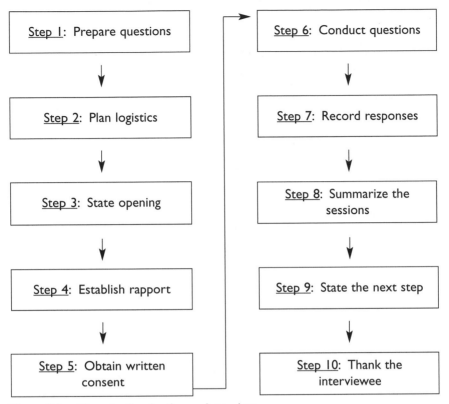

Figure 3.9.   Steps in Conducting an Interview

to pilot the questions with a small group of experts or respondents before the interview session.

In step two, the researcher should plan the *logistics* for the session. It
is important to find a suitable location for the interviewee(s) so that they
will feel comfortable. This location should be in a quiet place with little
distractions or potential for interruptions. For example, if the researcher
selects the teacher's office or administrator's office, the student might
feel very uncomfortable, given that it is not familiar territory. It might be
more practical to find a neutral location, such as the student's study hall
or classroom.

The third step of the interview involves the *opening*. Here, the researcher needs to set the stage regarding the purpose of the session and
the ground rules, such as: it is an informal interview, the respondent
should answer questions candidly and honestly, and state the time

length of the interview. The fourth step involves *establishing rapport* with the interviewee. It is crucial that the researcher always be courteous and try to obtain the trust of the interviewee. Without this trust, it is very difficult to obtain the desired information and data. A simple approach in establishing rapport might be for the researcher to begin by simply asking the interviewee how he or she feels about participating in this session. The interviewer can then give his or her own feelings about past participation in interviews as a way to develop common ground. The interviewer might also extend appreciation to the interviewee for taking his or her time for the session or complimenting the interviewee for his or her participation.

Step five involves *obtaining a written consent* from the interviewee, which gives permission for the interview session. The consent form should contain information regarding confidentiality, anonymity, privacy, benefits of the research, purpose of the information, intentions of the study, and the fact that the session is voluntary. The interviewer might also offer to give the interviewee a copy of the questions or study when completed. Asking the interviewee for a written consent is best obtained after rapport has been established. Otherwise, the interviewee might be more reluctant to agree to the consent form and the interview session might need to be aborted.

Step six consists of the researcher *asking the questions*. It is important that the interviewer avoid asking leading questions (i.e., questions that bias the interviewee's responses) so that the interviewee can give his or her candid responses without influence from the interviewer. There are several methods of asking questions (Figure 3.10).

Open-ended questions are structured so that the interviewee is forced to respond with one or more statements. Examples include, "What did you like about the lesson today?" and "What are the things

▶ Open-ended questions
▶ Closed-ended questions
▶ Paraphrasing
▶ Reflection
▶ Use of expanders
▶ Silence

Figure 3.10.   Examples of Questioning Techniques

you like best about your teacher?" Open-ended questions can be very powerful in obtaining a lot of information from the interviewee, although it can be ineffective and time consuming if the interviewer only is concerned with a yes or no response. *Close-ended questions* are best when the interviewer desires a brief "yes or no" answer. Typical closed-ended questions are "Did you like the lesson?" and "Do you like your teacher?"

The use of *paraphrasing* can be a useful questioning technique when the research interviewer desires the interviewee to elaborate. The paraphrasing technique consists of the interviewer simply putting in his or her own words what the interviewee stated. This can be good in drawing out additional information from the interviewee. *Reflection* is an interviewing technique that simply consists of a restatement of the interviewee's comment. For example, if the interviewee states that he or she feels sad in class, the interviewer would simply respond by saying, "You feel sad in class?" Restatement techniques can force the interviewee to continue talking and elaborate.

The use of the *expanders* are simply short words or expressions that the interviewer can state that will cause the interviewee to continue talking. Examples include; "Go on," "I see," "Is that right?" "Okay," and "Good." The last technique, the use of *silence*, might appear ironic as a questioning technique, but sometimes the best questioning technique is to not ask a question at all. The use of silence can force the interviewee to begin talking and can be more powerful in gaining information than asking structured questions that could stifle the interviewee from freely talking.

The last steps in the process consist of recording the responses, summarizing the session, stating the next step in the research process, and thanking the interviewee for participating in the interview. The researcher should always give his or her best estimates for completing the study so that the participants do not develop unrealistic expectations.

Group Interviews   There are several methods in conducting interviews. The *group interview* is one that consists of asking questions to two or more people who have gathered for a session. It is important to select people who can make a contribution to the interview session. Otherwise, one or more people misselected can interfere with the interviewing process and the researcher will fail to get good results. The interview process has been popular for many fields of study, such as sociologists, psychologists, educators, and health-care professionals. Conducting a group interview requires a great deal of skill by the interviewer. He or she needs to be able to pay attention to all the participants of the group and ensure that everyone contributes. The interviewer needs to have good facilitation skills in controlling the dominating individuals and drawing out responses from shy individuals.

There are several types of difficult participants in a group interview (Figure 3.11). The *excessive complainer* is the type of interviewee who takes advantage of the session by expressing his or her negative feelings. These complainers have a certain characteristic sound. If you listen to them, it sounds almost melodic. They also use a lot of "ands" and "buts." Complainers often have the ability to switch from one topic to another without hardly taking a breath. Although the interviewer might gain a lot of information, the complainer generally gets off topic and needs to be controlled. In essence, complainers are people who develop a sense of powerlessness. They often see causes of their problems as being outside influences, such as fate or other people. Therefore, when problems are encountered, the complainers are more apt to blame others than to accept it and try to logically understand the root cause of problems. In dealing with complainers, try not to produce an adversarial relationship. The researcher might start by paraphrasing or restatement such as "Okay, I understand," or "Let me see if I can paraphrase this." The researcher should also try not to apologize for the complainer's excessive complaints, but rather try to move to problem solving with the complainer to gain the information needed.

The *hostile interviewee* can be difficult to control. This individual is generally abrupt, abrasive, and emotional. The hostile person is not the most common type of interviewee, but certainly is one of the most difficult to manage. They generally have a deep sense of feelings about the way others should behave and there is often a noticeable degree of anger and distortion of real facts. They are generally inconsiderate to the interviewer. The hostile individual also has a very negative attitude and sometimes believes that outside influences are overwhelming. They often disregard the positive aspects and tend to focus only on the negative. They reinforce this attitude until it often becomes a consistent pattern. It

Type of Difficult Interviewee: The excessive complainer interviewee

➡ *Managing Technique:*

- State, "I understand your feelings"
- Don't reinforce
- Ignore the complaint

Type of Difficult Interviewee: The abusive interviewee

➡ *Managing Technique:*

- Don't argue
- Stick to the facts
- Be firm but let them save face

Type of Difficult Interviewee: The long-winded interviewee

➡ *Managing Technique:*

- Paraphrase
- Provide restatement
- Don't reinforce
- Interrupt and suggest specific response

Type of Difficult Interviewee: The shy interviewee

➡ *Managing Technique:*

- Ask open-ended questions
- Use paraphrasing techniques
- Use expanders

Type of Difficult Interviewee: The drifter interviewee

➡ *Managing Technique:*

- Don't reinforce
- Say, "I understand," and redirect
- Stick to the interview topic

Figure 3.11.   Handling Difficult Interviewees

is essential that when dealing with a hostile interviewee the researcher does not develop an adversarial relationship. He or she should give direct eye contact, de-escalate any conflict or negativity, and should not be overly polite.

The *long-winded interviewee* can disrupt the entire group by not allowing others to speak and often gives a biased view of the group's opinions. This person often comes across as a know-it-all. He or she is generally very confident and appears to have all the answers, and often generalizes about the problem from a biased viewpoint. In dealing with them, the researcher should make statements like, "I appreciate your responses, now can I hear other opinions, too?" Also, the interviewer can use paraphrase and restatement techniques to help control this dominating person.

The *shy interviewee* can be difficult for the interviewer to extract information. This person often feels uncomfortable giving opinions in a group setting and might be hard to understand. He or she might have a sense of mistrust and feel embarrassed giving information in a group setting. Therefore, in managing this type of interviewee it is important to use open-ended questions, paraphrasing, and expander techniques.

The *drifter interviewee* is the type of person who takes discussion off track. This individual might focus on personal issues rather than the topic of the interview session. The interviewee might want to take advantage of the session for hidden agendas or personal motives. In dealing with this type of interviewee it is important to redirect the individual to the topic and not reinforce this behavior.

Focus Groups   A special type of group interview is called a *focus group*. A focus group generally consists of about five to ten people, who are interviewed in a comfortable, nonthreatening setting. Although the interviewer might ask questions to the focus group, the participants often just share their feelings and perceptions while the interviewer records their responses. The focus group might also have an internal facilitator who helps to direct questions or record their responses. Sometimes responses can actually be recorded on a flip chart or newsprint. The interview questions can be placed on the top of several flip chart sheets and, when filled with responses, taped to the wall so that everyone can see the information.

Although there are different variations of conducting a focus group, the most common, from an action research standpoint, is to ask questions to the members and then record their responses. It is important to allow the participants to have freedom and responsibility for eliciting responses from everyone within their group. The focus group operates best when all members have a common interest and are genuinely interested in obtaining everyone's views within the group. It also is important to select several participants for the group so that there are enough people to provide a representative sample, but a group that is not too large to stifle discussion. In preparing questions for the focus group, the interviewer could first develop a set of questions and then pilot the set of questions with experts or one or two individuals to ensure that the questions are appropriate. Figure 3.12 gives an example of questions that could be asked to a focus group on the topic of discipline.

Individual Interviews Conducting the individual interview takes different skills than conducting a group interview. Conducting an interview with one person can be valuable in drawing out true feelings that might not be obtained in a group setting. Because the goal in action research is to solve problems, it might be necessary to conduct an individual session because the root problem could be with just one person. For example, if a student has a disciplinary problem, the researcher might need to conduct a counseling session with the student to resolve the issue (Tomal, 1999). Although the process of asking questions might be similar in an individual interview as in a group interview, one variation to the interview process is called the *coaching session* (Figure 3.13).

- ▶ How do you feel about the use of corporal punishment?
- ▶ How important is due process?
- ▶ Do you believe schools should use a zero tolerance policy?
- ▶ Should mitigating circumstances be considered in giving disciplinary action?
- ▶ Do you believe in progressive discipline?
- ▶ What is the teacher's responsibility and authority in administering discipline?
- ▶ How should discipline be administered to students with disabilities?
- ▶ Where should the disciplinary session be administered?
- ▶ What is the relationship between school discipline and search procedures?
- ▶ What are some legal aspects in administering discipline?
- ▶ How should schools deal with violent offenders?
- ▶ How should a school develop a uniform policy?
- ▶ What are reasons for disciplining students?
- ▶ Should counseling be a first step to the discipline procedure?
- ▶ Do you think peer mediation programs work?
- ▶ What is the role of parents in school discipline?

Figure 3.12.   Example of Group Interview Questions. Focus Group Topic: Discipline

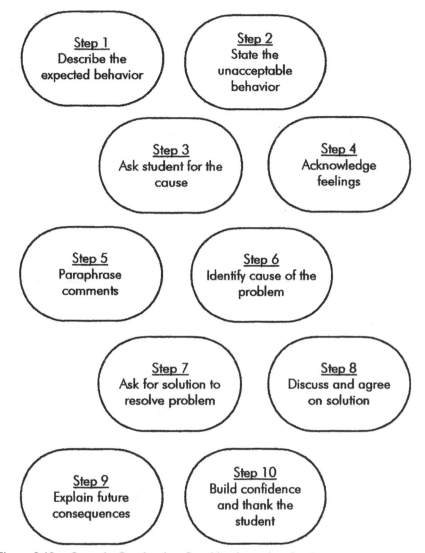

Figure 3.13. Steps in Conducting Coaching Interview Session

Step one of the coaching session begins by describing the *expected behavior*. The teacher should start the session by explaining the process, describing the expected behavior required of all students, and stating the school policy. Too often, teachers are quick to blame a student for an issue without first describing the school's policy and expectation for good student behavior. By stating the expected *behavior standard*, the teacher confirms the school's policy on performance expectations.

In step two, the teacher should state the *unacceptable behavior*. The teacher should describe the student's misbehavior in a neutral, but firm, manner. He or she should give specific examples and actual facts to support the allegation. Documentation as well as statements by witnesses can also be helpful in supporting the allegation. During this step, the teacher should be careful not to personally belittle or degrade the student or create an intimidating atmosphere.

Step three consists of asking the student the *cause of the problem*. It is important that the teacher consider possible causes that could have contributed to the misbehavior, such as: peer influence, home environment, aptitude, attitude, motivation, or health conditions (e.g., behavioral or learning disability). Often if the teacher considers these causes, there is a good chance that one of them will be the root cause of the student's problem. During this step, it is also important that the student acknowledge his or her responsibility for his or her actions (Tomal, 1999).

In step four, the teacher needs to *listen* to the student and then *acknowledge* the student's feelings. Whether the teacher agrees or not with the student, it is important that the teacher give his or her full attention to the student, empathize with the student, and maintain rapport. The student might express remorse, anger, or hostility. The teacher might respond by stating "I understand how you feel in this situation" or "I see how someone would have feelings like this in this situation." Recognizing the student's feelings helps to personalize the conversation and develop rapport, which can help in resolving the issue. Even if the student is perceived as being cold and indifferent, the teacher still needs to recognize his or her feelings.

The next step involves *paraphrasing* the student's statement so that the teacher can confirm and document the actual comments made by the student. This technique also helps to promote further discussion so that the issue can be resolved. In step six, the teacher should *identify the cause of the problem*. This step often entails an in-depth discussion because students are often reluctant to give the cause or they have not thought about the reason for their misbehavior. Step seven involves solving the problem. It is best to begin by asking the student for solutions. The students are more likely to change their behavior if they have participated in the solution. For example, if the student suggests an appropriate solution to the problem, and it is agreeable to the teacher, then the teacher should agree with the student. If a student suggests a solution that is inappropriate, then the teacher needs to further discuss the problem and consider offering his or her own *solution* (step eight). If the student is unwilling to consider any reasonable option, then the teacher will have no choice but to impose his or her own solution to the problem.

Step nine involves *indicating future consequences* for continued misbehavior. This step requires that the teacher explain the consequences of misbehavior and ensure that the student recognizes the further consequences. The last step involves *supporting the student and building confidence*. It is crucial that the teacher reinforce a positive atmosphere and state to the student that he or she can improve. Although it might be difficult at times for teachers to give this support, an attempt to restore a positive working relationship is crucial to resolving the issue and making improvements. Teachers should also use appropriate body language. The subtle nonverbal cues and signals that a student notices can communicate a teacher's feelings toward a student. Last, the teacher should *thank the student* for participating in the individual interview session. The teacher might want to document the results of the session, which could be necessary for future actions (Tomal, 1999).

The effective interviewer is one who can quickly establish rapport with the interviewee and obtain relevant information. One of the more practical theories in helping an interviewer in communicating with a person is the use of personality styles. The theory of personality styles is as outgrowth of the work of Carl Gustav Jung. Jung, a Swiss psychoanalyst, and student and colleague of Sigmund Freud, articulated the basic theory of personality (Jung, 1923). He believed that people had four personality styles and that most individuals have a dominant personality style genetically determined and can even be observed at the infant stage. As an outgrowth of Jung's work, four styles were identified called: intuitor, feeler, thinker, and doer (Tomal, 1999).

The *intuitor* personality style has communication characteristics of being theoretical, abstract, introspective, conceptional, and tends to communicate with respect of the time frame of the future. They place an emphasis on ingenuity, creativity, and originality. Intuitors are often verbose, intuitive, imaginative, and expressive during interview sessions.

They tend to communicate in a unique, novel, or conceptual manner. However, although intuitors appear to be insightful, they are often criticized for being impractical or unorganized. Therefore, the interviewer might need to keep the interview structured.

The *feeler* personality style is one who values feelings and emotions of people. During an interview, feelers are often very personal, good listeners, and tend to be very respectful to the interviewer. They also might exhibit behaviors of being perceptive, sensitive, warm, and empathetic. Given that feelers are people oriented, they may also come across as spontaneous and introspective during the interview. However, at their worst they can be seen as impulsive, overdramatic, moody, and emotional. Therefore, it is important to ask a variety of well-rounded questions because they tend to focus on people, feelings, and emotions.

The *thinker* personality style tends to have characteristics of being objective, logical, and analytical during the interview session. Thinkers can be effective in organizing their thoughts and presenting them in a clear and detailed manner. However, they tend to be indecisive in answering questions and prefer to ponder information for a long period of time instead of making a quick decision. Their strengths during interview sessions include being deliberate, objective, and analytical. Their weaknesses include being too rigid, overcautious, controlling, systematic, and stoic.

The *doer* personality style is practical and results oriented. During the interview doers will probably communicate in short and to-the-point statements. They are less likely to engage in personal collaborative discussions that are emotionally based. The doers strength include characteristics of being pragmatic, efficient, and straightforward in giving responses. However, their weaknesses include characteristics of being too combative, demanding, impatient, insensitive, and short-sighted.

Understanding the use of the personality styles can help the interviewer in conducting interview sessions (Figure 3.14). For example, individuals with similar styles tend to communicate more effectively with each other. They tend to "talk the language" of the other person. However, two people (i.e., interviewer and interviewee) with dissimilar personality styles might encounter miscommunication. For example, if the interviewer tends to be a thinker and he or she is interviewing a personality who is dominantly an intuitor, the interviewer might appear to the person as being overly controlling and lacking ingenuity. The inter-

Personality Style: Intuitor
➡ *Characteristics:*

- Be enthusiastic
- Focus on creativity and innovation
- Allow for flexibility and freedom

Personality Style: Feeler
➡ *Characteristics:*

- Personalize discussion
- Be concerned with feelings, uniqueness, and individuality
- Relate experiences based on emotional reactions, feelings, warmth and empathy

Personality Style: Thinker
➡ *Characteristics:*

- Present information in an organized, structured manner
- Don't push for immediate action and responses
- Be logical and data oriented and present things in a logical fashion
- Be more analytical and quantitative

Personality Style: Doer
➡ *Characteristics:*

- Be practical and concrete, spirited, and down to earth
- Use physical, practical examples in discussions and be succinct in questioning

Figure 3.14.   Personality Styles During Interview Sessions

viewer might overwhelm the interviewee and he or she may not listen or actively participate.

On the other hand, if the interviewer is a doer personality style and the interviewee has an intuitor style, conflict could arise. The interviewer might be viewed as being too impulsive, quick, and bottom-line oriented. The interviewee might become frustrated and impatient and desire a more creative, innovative, or animated approach to the interview session, instead of being too down-to-earth and succinct.

The use of personality styles can be a useful aide when conducting interviewing sessions. The key to communicating effectively with interviewees begins with identifying one's own dominant style and then the style of the other person. This does not mean that the interviewer must permanently change, but rather adapt one's approach to the interviewee(s). For example, when interviewing a person who is a dominant thinker, extra time might need to be taken to organize the questions and talk in a structured manner. When approaching an intuitor, an interviewer might want to be more dynamic and offer more thought-provoking statements. When dealing with a thinker, the discussion should be more structured and organized and presented in a step-by-step fashion. The feeler might also need time to contemplate and process information as compared to the doer, who might be more inclined to give his or her opinions. Doers, however, might just want to give quick answers to questions and the interview session may be short-changed in getting in-depth information.

One of the potential difficult aspects a person might encounter during an individual interview is defensiveness. When people become defensive, they often resort to using *defense mechanisms*. Defense mechanisms are psychological crutches that people utilize to prevent themselves from experiencing negative feelings (Figure 3.15).

Denial is a defense mechanism where people simply deny their own behaviors or feelings about a situation. For example, if a person is asked an uncomfortable question during the interview, he or she might give an untruthful response rather than experience potential embarrassment. *Projection* is a technique where an individual transfers his or her feelings to another person. For example, a student might state, "I am not tired, she is tired," or "I'm not disorganized, you are disorganized." It is important for the interviewer to watch for these patterns in people, which can give clues to their actual feelings and to ask follow up questions to gain clarification or verification of their responses. The use of *reaction formation* is

> ▸ Denial
> ▸ Projection
> ▸ Reaction formation
> ▸ Fantasy and idealization
> ▸ Avoidance
> ▸ Aggressive behavior
> ▸ Displacement

Figure 3.15. Defense Mechanisms Used During Interview Sessions

a defense mechanism used when the interviewee states the total opposite of what he or she feels. For example, instead of stating that the student dislikes class, he or she might say that class is enjoyable. This is a way to prevent the student from facing his or her true feelings and experiencing negative feelings. The use of *fantasy and idealization* is a defense mechanism in which students have unrealistic opinions. They might fantasize about others (e.g., movie stars, music performers) and give responses during the interview based upon their ideal perceptions of themselves.

The use of *avoidance* is a very common technique where people simply avoid answering questions rather than face their true feelings. During the interview session, an interviewer might encounter aggressive behavior. In this situation, the interviewer should be sure to establish rapport and always give courtesy and respect to the interviewee. The use of *displacement* is a technique whereby a student blames another student or take his or her negative feelings and transfers them to another person. The student might make statements such as, "I don't like my fellow student; she is always teasing me." Student use this technique to save face rather than take ownership for their own behavior.

Structured Interviews Structured interviews are sometimes called *formal interviews*. This interview consists of predetermined questions. The structured interview can be an efficient process, although it does not allow for flexibility in gaining information. The questions tend to be closed-ended questions that require a yes or no answer or a short response. Generally, the interviewee is not allowed to follow up with providing additional information that could be relevant. The structured interview is similar to asking a set of questions based on items from a questionnaire. The typical telephone interview is a common example of a structured interview session.

A variation of the structured interview is the unstructured approach. The types of questions used in this interview allow for a great deal of latitude for the interviewee. Interviewers tend to ask open-ended questions, such as "What classes did you like best in school?," "Which were your favorite teachers and why?," "How did your teachers make learning interesting?," and "What were some of the most rewarding experiences in school?" These questions often provide rich and in-depth responses. For example, if conducting an unstructured interview session with a group of students concerning what motivates them in class, the questions include:

"Do you feel motivated by learning the material itself?," "Does recognition motivate you?," "Does the use of rewards provide incentive for motivation?," and "What things demotivate you from wanting to learn?"

SURVEYING

Conducting a survey is, without a doubt, one of the most popular and effective techniques for data collection in action research. A survey is used to obtain opinions from people regarding their feelings, beliefs, impressions, and facts about almost any educational issue or problem. Although different formats are used in conducting a survey, the main objective is to ask questions directly to people to get information that can be later analyzed and then used to develop action plans to address educational issues. Although most surveys tend to be administered through a questionnaire to a large number of people, surveys can also be conducted on an individual basis and administered through the Internet, over the telephone, via fax, or in person.

Group Surveys

Traditionally, surveys have been used when there is a large number of people in the sample population when conducting personal interviews would be impractical and time consuming. This survey is called a *group survey*. However, the use of the survey has evolved in action research, and is used for many different purposes, such as: surveying a person, an entire classroom of students, the teachers and parents, or all stakeholders of a school district. Figure 3.16 shows an example of some of the topics in which surveys have been used to obtain information.

Although surveys have many uses, they can be especially helpful in conducting longitudinal and trend studies. These types of studies collect information at different points in time and when assessing different samples from populations whose participants have changed and the researcher wants to make a comparison. Surveys can also be useful as a follow up to implementing actions to evaluate the results of the actions. The use of surveys can not always determine valid changes because the survey has been administered at different points of time historically. Although, the

▶ Determining attitudes of adolescent student reading instruction
▶ Assessing teachers' opinions regarding class size reduction program
▶ Determining if time-out techniques are effective in enforcing discipline rules
▶ Assessing parents' opinions regarding gifted placement program
▶ Determining the effectiveness of lap-top computers on standardized test scores
▶ Assessing special education teachers' attitudes toward inclusion
▶ Identifying health program practices for early Head Start programs
▶ Identifying qualitative learning techniques on mathematical achievement
▶ Assessing the impact of character education on student performance

Figure 3.16.   Example of Action Research Topics for Using Surveys

information can be helpful in supporting the action researcher's opinions in evaluating actions. For example, a principal could administer a survey to assess the opinions of teachers regarding the operations of the school. She could then implement actions for school improvements and then re-assess the teachers' opinions with a follow-up survey. Because the surveys are administered at different points in time, other external factors could influence the teachers' opinions. However, the information from the two surveys can be compared and be valuable in helping the principal in his assessment. Likewise, a teacher could administer a survey to all of her students regarding her teaching style. The teacher can then assess the students' opinions, implement actions to make instructional improvement, and then administer a follow-up survey to assess the results. This form of action research can be valuable in assisting a teacher in collecting information in an anonymous and confidential manner. Students will be more likely to give candid and honest responses if a survey is used, rather than through personal interviews with the teacher. Given that action research is less exact and precise than scientific research, it is important that an action researcher resist the temptation to be careless.

The process of conducting a survey should be systematic and thorough. Typical problems in conducting a survey consist of improperly defining the population, neglecting to establish sufficient resources prior to starting the survey, failing to pilot the questionnaire, and being too hasty is designing the items for the questionnaire (Figure 3.17).

For example, a common problem in administering a survey is the action researcher's failure to properly plan for the entire sequence of events. For example, if the survey is administered to a large group of

  ▶ Improperly identifying the target population
  ▶ Poor planning of resources
  ▶ Poor design of questionnaire items
  ▶ Failing to pilot the questionnaire
  ▶ Poor planning of survey administration
  ▶ Failing to properly decide data analysis prior to administration
  ▶ Failing to consider all questions that need to be addressed

Figure 3.17.   Problems in Conducting Surveys

participants and a problem in the questionnaire is discovered, then the entire survey might need to be redone. This problem can be prevented if the questionnaire is first pilot tested with a small group. Another common problem is the failure to have a precise plan of analyzing the data prior to administering the questionnaire. Without a clear and defined process for analyzing the data, the researcher might need to construct the items on the questionnaire differently than if the researcher had planned better. Figure 3.18 lists the steps in conducting a survey.

Step one in conducting a survey is *identifying the problem*. The action researcher must first identify the educational problem and what he or she would like to improve. Generally, this requires writing a well-defined statement of the problem. For example, the researcher might desire to improve the instructional skills of teachers, the math achievement of students, or the morale of students in a classroom. This first step allows the researcher to decide on the actual objectives of the survey and determine if the survey is the best method for addressing the problem. If the researcher wants to identify the skill areas in need of staff development in order to design a suitable training workshop, then a survey might be an appropriate approach. However, if the researcher would like to improve the disciplinary behavior of a student, a survey might not be appropriate, versus conducting an interview with the students. Likewise, if a researcher is concerned with improving the math achievement of students, he or she can assess the students' level of math proficiency and then administer an action step to approve their ability rather than administering a survey, which would be of little value. In identifying the problem definition, some possible questions the researcher can ask include: "What is the educational problem?," "What is the intended outcome?," "Will a survey be the best method for collecting data?," Should

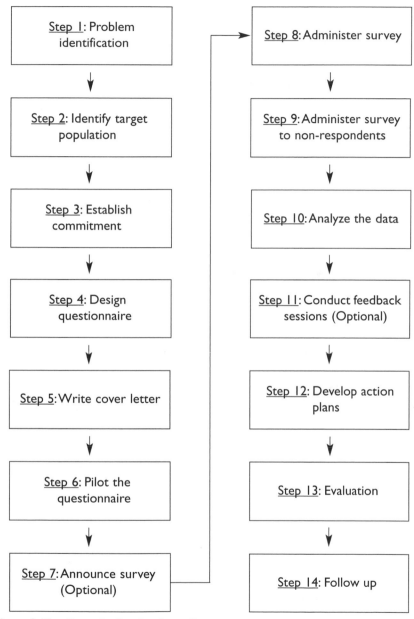

Figure 3.18. Steps in Conducting a Survey

another intervention method be used along with the questionnaire?," and "What is the time frame available to conduct the survey?"

Once the researcher has defined the problem, he or she must clearly *identify the target population* (step two). The exact participants to be included in the survey administration need to be identified. For example, if a researcher desires to administer a survey to a group of bilingual children, a survey questionnaire might be inappropriate if the children have a difficult time in understanding vocabulary or if their reading level is not proficient. In this case, although a survey might initially seem to be the most effective means, the researcher could decide to conduct interviews with the children rather than obtain information through a questionnaire. Also, administering a questionnaire to a target population when the subjects have little knowledge about the topic might be futile. For example, if a graduate student is seeking to assess an educational program and decides to administer a questionnaire to all the teachers, this process will likely be ineffective if the teachers are unfamiliar with the educational program. Upon analyzing the results, the graduate student might find that most of the questionnaires were returned without being completed. Therefore, understanding the target population and ensuring that the participants have the proficiency and knowledge to answer the items on the questionnaire are basic to all survey administration.

Another example of administering a survey without completely understanding the target population involves a situation of an education consultant desiring to improve teacher morale problems within a school district. The consultant might administer an organizational survey to all the teachers to assess their opinions about the school, only to find that the majority of teachers strongly agreed to all the statements. The consultant might later discover that the superintendent's office was desiring to remove the principal and most of the teachers were supporting the principal and decided to rate every statement very high so that the overall results of the survey would appear very favorable to the principal. Therefore, in this situation, obviously, the administration of the survey was ineffective, given the politics within the school district.

Step three consists of ensuring that there is *commitment* to conduct the survey. For example, a researcher might feel that a survey is the most appropriate intervention for collecting data, but that the resources are inadequate to administer it. For example, if a consultant is interested in administering a survey to assess the teacher professional development needs, she must first talk to the administration to ensure that the resources are adequate, such as: people to administer the survey, money for making copies of the questionnaire and postage, time for teachers to complete the questionnaire, computer equipment and software to complete the analysis of the data, and time for the teachers to hear the results of the survey and participate in developing action plans to address the issues. For example, it is unrealistic to administer a survey if the teachers are too busy with more important activities. For example, teachers might be too busy at the start of the school year and too stressed at the end of the school year to give meaningful and unbiased opinions. Also, if the teachers are too busy or have higher priorities, it might result in a low turn out in completion of the survey. Therefore, in establishing commitment, the researcher must consider all time frames, logistics, allocation of resources, and realistic goals and deadlines for the survey administration.

The *design of the questionnaire* (step four) can be the trickiest part of the whole survey process. If the researcher doesn't develop a quality questionnaire, the result of the survey will be poor. The actual questionnaire, sometimes called the *instrument,* can be designed by using some basic guidelines (Figure 3.19).

Two types of questions can be used for the questionnaire: closed-ended questions and open-ended questions. Closed-ended questions are similar to multiple choice questions, which allow the respondent to select or rate a numerical value for the question. The answers to the questions typically measure the respondent's attitude, knowledge, or opinion. Many different

▸ Use common language; avoid jargon
▸ Keep the questionnaire short, but without losing substance
▸ Select the best scale for rating items
▸ Include specific, thorough directions
▸ Number each of the pages and statements
▸ Develop an attractive questionnaire format
▸ Don't mix positive and negative statements, which can confuse respondents
▸ Avoid leading questions that cause the respondents to answer in a preferred way
▸ Avoid repetitive statements
▸ Include specific instructions for returning the questionnaire

Figure 3.19. Guidelines in Designing Questionnaires

Forced Choice Learning

Directions: Circle the number that represents the extent to your agreement or disagreement for each of the questions:

▶ Problem-based learning improves my understanding of science.
  Extent of agreement (circle one)

  1. Strongly agree
  2. Agree
  3. Disagree
  4. Strongly disagree

Figure 3.20.   Example of Close-ended Questions and Questionnaire Scales

types of scales can be used for closed-ended questions. Selecting the best scale is crucial for allowing the respondent to easily answer each of the questions and for the researcher to later analyze the data. For example, if the researcher desires the respondent to make a forced decision among items that are similar, he or she might want to use the forced ranking scale (Figure 3.20). A *forced ranking scale* can be good to use to ensure that the respondent is forced into making a decision among several items.

In some instances, a simple *yes or no scale* is the most effective and least confusing. These scales offer a quick and easy method for the participants in answering questions (Figure 3.21).

Another type of questionnaire scale is the *graphic ratings scale*. This scale can be useful when a wide degree of assessment is desired. This scale is especially useful when rating similar items (Figure 3.22).

Of the many types of scales, the *Likert scale*, named after Rensis Likert, is one of the more popular scales that uses a five-point scale ranging from "strongly agree" to "strongly disagree" (Figure 3.23).

Directions: Circle the answer that indicates your opinion regarding the following statement:

▶ I enjoy reading at home in my spare time.
  1. Yes
  2. No

▶ I enjoy my reading assignments.
  1. Yes
  2. No

Figure 3.21.   Example of Yes-No Responses

Directions: Please mark an "x" on the line which indicates your opinion about your teacher's effectiveness.

- ▸ Giving Instructions

  1　2　3　4　5　6　7　8　9
  Very   Very
  effective   ineffective

- ▸ Answering student questions

  1　2　3　4　5　6　7　8　9
  Very   Very
  effective   ineffective

- ▸ Explaining homework

  1　2　3　4　5　6　7　8　9
  Very   Very
  effective   ineffective

Figure 3.22. Graphic Ratings Scale for Assessing Teacher Effectiveness

The five-point scale is most common, but there are many other types and categories of scales (see Figure 3.24).

One of the more challenging questionnaires to design is when working with people with limited reading or comprehension ability, such as special education or early childhood students. It might be difficult for

Directions: Please indicate your extent of agreement for each of the items by circling the number:

- ▸ I believe students feel safe and secure at school

  1　　　2　　　3　　　4　　　5
  Strongly   Agree   Undecided   Disagree   Strongly
  Agree   Disagree

- ▸ I believe morale is high with students

  1　　　2　　　3　　　4　　　5
  Strongly   Agree   Undecided   Disagree   Strongly
  Agree   Disagree

Rank Order Scale

Directions: Please rank the four subjects based upon how valuable they are in life.

1　　　2　　　3　　　4　　　5
Most   Least
Important   Important

- ▸ Mathematics _____
- ▸ Reading _____
- ▸ Science _____
- ▸ Spelling _____

Figure 3.23.   Examples of a Likert Questionnaire Scale

Category 1	Category 2	Category 3	Category 4
Strongly disagree	Very favorable	Strongly approve	Very frequently
Disagree	Favorable	Approve	Frequently
Undecided	Neither favorable	Neither approve	Sometimes
Agree	or unfavorable	or disapprove	Almost never
Strongly agree	Unfavorable	Disapprove	
	Very unfavorable	Strongly disagree	

Figure 3.24. Categories of Scales

students with special needs or young children to completely understand the statements or scale. Therefore, one practical scale is the *facial pictorial scale* (Figure 3.25). When using the facial pictorial scale it may be necessary to read the questions and ask the student to point to each of the faces representing each of their responses.

A combination of different scales can be useful in surveys. For example, a combination of a categorical scale with an open-ended forced ranking can be useful in allowing the respondents to make thorough analysis of their ratings by completing this two-stage approach (Figure 3.26).

In the first stage, the categorical rating scale, the participants rate the factors, depending upon their extent of agreement for each item. For example, if the participants are rating the importance of the different topics for their personal development, this scale allows the respondents to rate each of the factors. After the respondents have rated each of the factors, then he or she completes the second stage by force

Directions: Please point to the face that represents your feelings towards each of the questions.

> ▸ I like to read
> ▸ I like my teacher
> ▸ I like my classmates
> ▸ I like my school books
> ▸ I like my school
> ▸ I like my principal
> ▸ I like my classroom

Figure 3.25.   Example of a Facial Pictorial Scale

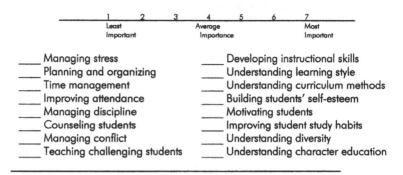

Directions: The purpose of this assessment is to assist Human Resources in selecting the most appropriate professional development topics. Please assign a number from one to seven for each of the topic indicating the degree of need for your further professional development.

	1	2	3	4	5	6	7	
	Least Important			Average Importance			Most Important	

____ Managing stress   ____ Developing instructional skills
____ Planning and organizing ____ Understanding learning style
____ Time management   ____ Understanding curriculum methods
____ Improving attendance   ____ Building students' self-esteem
____ Managing discipline   ____ Motivating students
____ Counseling students   ____ Improving student study habits
____ Managing conflict   ____ Understanding diversity
____ Teaching challenging students ____ Understanding character education

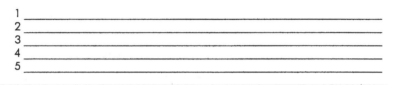

Directions: Please rank order from the above or other topics, the five topics most needed for your professional development (1 is most important).

1 _____
2 _____
3 _____
4 _____
5 _____

Figure 3.26. Sample Professional Development Questionaire Using a Two-stage Scale (Categorical Scale and Forced Ranking Scale)

ranking which of the top five factors would be most useful for his or her professional development. In this way, the researcher obtains two sets of data with which to analyze and make conclusions. The second set of data, the forced ranking factors, would probably receive more importance given that they were based upon previous analysis by the respondent (Figure 3.26).

There is an old saying that when a person is trying to secure employment that the purpose of the resume is to get the interview. Likewise, in survey administration, the purpose of the *cover letter* (step five) is to get the respondent to complete the questionnaire. Therefore, in both cases, each one needs to be written in a manner to accomplish the objective. Although the letter should be succinct, it should also contain all the necessary information the respondents need to accurately complete the questionnaire (Figure 3.27).

▶ Is the purpose of questionnaire stated?
▶ Is the importance of study emphasized?
▶ Is the study anonymous?
▶ Will the data be confidential?
▶ Does an informed consent form need to be enclosed?
▶ Does the study need to be described?
▶ Is the study voluntary?
▶ Will the respondents get a copy of the results?
▶ What is the time table for the study?
▶ Did you thank the respondents?

Figure 3.27.   Questions to Consider in Designing a Cover Letter

Most cover letters should explain exactly the purpose of the study, what will happen to the data, and if the respondent is anonymous. The researcher needs also to be concerned with any sensitive areas or politics in completing the questionnaire. For example, a consultant was once asked to administer a school survey to all the teachers in a district office because there were several disgruntled teachers who disapproved of the principal's performance. Therefore, a discussion with the consultant, principal, and district superintendent was held to determine who should sign the cover letter in announcing the survey. If only the principal signed the letter, then many of the teachers would think that the survey process is biased toward the principal and the teachers would not trust the process. If only the consultant signed the cover letter, the importance of the entire survey would not be valued by the teachers if the school administration is not involved. Also, if only the superintendent were to sign the cover letter then teachers might also feel apprehensive given the principal is not involved, or an unbiased third party consultant. In this particular case, it was decided that all three people, the principal, the consultant, and the superintendent would draft a letter together and sign it so that the teachers would understand that everyone is involved in this process. Therefore, before administering a survey, all potential concerns and issues in drafting the letter as well as the questionnaire should be explored to ensure that the respondents will complete the questionnaire with candidness and honesty. (Figure 3.28 shows a sample cover letter.)

Some researchers have developed creative techniques in designing cover letters to increase the rate of return. For example, some people en-

Dear Teachers and Staff,

We are interested in obtaining your opinions regarding our school and would appreciate if you would complete the enclosed questionnaire and return it in the stamped, self-addressed envelope by March 15, 2003. The survey is being conducted by Dr. Smith, an independent consultant, who will complete the analysis and then conduct a feedback session for all teachers to explain the results of the survey. Based upon the results of the survey, I would like to establish quality teams to address the issues for our school.

The questionnaire is completely anonymous and voluntary. Your individual responses to the questionnaire will remain strictly confidential. Also, informed consent procedures for this study are contained in the questionnaire. Please take a moment to read it.

Thank you for your cooperation and participation in this process. I look forward to meeting with you during the feedback session.

Sincerely,

Mr. Jones

Mr. Jones
Principal

Enclosure

Figure 3.28.   Example of a Cover Letter

close a small cash incentive or promise a gift for completing the questionnaire. Generally, if a cash reward is enclosed such as a few dollars, it should be clear that the money is being offered as a token of appreciation rather than for the respondent's performance in completing the survey. This will help ensure that the survey process is unbiased. The researcher should also include a date on which the questionnaire needs to be returned, otherwise people may procrastinate if a date is not given. The researcher should always include a stamped, self-addressed envelope, otherwise the rate of return will be decreased. The use of survey administration in action research probably has a higher rate of return than other types of research given that the respondents generally have a vested interested in solving educational problems and making improvements. The respondents are often individuals who desire to complete a questionnaire and be involved in developing action plans to address the issues. However, if the respondents feel that the survey is just another feeble attempt to gather information and that little will be done, their motivation will be low in completing the questionnaire. Therefore, when possible, the

administration and other influential people should sign the letter, which
will increase the rate of return.

A common mistake of researchers is their failure to properly *pilot the
questionnaire* before administering it (step six). Researchers should always pilot the questionnaire by pretesting it with a group of similar respondents. The researcher might conduct a focus group and read each
statement aloud and ask the respondents the meaning of each statement
and if each statement drives the intentions of the researcher. This
process will help to establish the validity and reliability of the statements
and allow the researcher to revise the statements as necessary. Another
method is to try two versions of the questionnaire on two different
subgroups and then make a comparison. When discussing each of the
questions with the focus group, pay close attention to the wording of
the statements to avoid biased or insensitive words. For example, if the
researcher administering the survey asks the respondents if they feel they
can trust people who have a beard, and if the researcher has a beard,
then obviously the responses will be biased. Likewise, certain words are
offensive, insensitive, or discriminatory against certain classes of people.
These words can be biased in terms of gender, age, ethnicity, race, sexual
orientation, or disability. For example, if a researcher is asking a group of
women faculty to answer a questionnaire regarding faculty development
and one of the statements refers to women as "girls" or "ladies," the respondents might be offended by the use of these potential "sexist" terms
and the results of the survey will be diminished. Also, for example, the
way in which some statements are worded can have a positive or negative impact on the responses. For example, a positively worded statement
might be "Do you feel we should provide funding for the poor?" versus
"Do you feel we should spend more taxes for welfare?" The first question
might generate a more favorable response than the latter.

In some situations, the researcher might want to *announce the administration of the survey* prior to actually distributing it (step seven). For example, if a principal is using a consultant to administer a school survey for
all the teachers, he or she might want to announce the survey a week in
advance so that teachers can be prepared to allocate time to complete the
survey and understand its importance. The teachers also might need time
to ask questions concerning the process prior to completing it. In other
cases, when a teacher is administering a survey to a class of students, he

or she might need to receive a signed consent form from their parents. In some cases, it is not necessary to announce the survey, such as in a case of department meeting where a small group of teachers will complete a survey for the department chairperson. In this situation, the chairperson could simply explain the purpose of the survey and then ask the teachers to complete it during the meeting, especially if it is a short questionnaire.

Step eight consists of *administering the survey*. The toughest part of administering the survey is when the group of participants is large. When the group is small, such as a class of students, then the sample population is considered self-contained and the researcher can easily administer the survey at one time and immediately collect the questionnaires. Difficulty can arise when the participants are not at one location and the researcher needs to mail the questionnaires. The use of mailed questionnaires always has a significantly lower rate of return than when the questionnaires are administered to one group in person. Likewise, when a questionnaire is used via the Internet, the rate of return can be lower even if follow up through e-mail is convenient. The best method of administering a questionnaire, when possible, is to administer the questionnaire in person to the group of participants. In this way, the researcher can explain the purpose of the study, give instructions in completing the questionnaire, and answer any of their questions. He or she can then allow a predetermined time for completing the questionnaire and then immediately pick up all the questionnaires.

When there is a significantly large group of people, then the researcher could obtain assistants to help administer the questionnaires. For example, a consultant once administered a questionnaire to 2,000 parents whose children attended one large school. Rather than mail the questionnaires to all 2,000 parents, given that the rate of return would most likely be lower, the researcher decided to use the students as a vehicle in administering the survey to their parents. The researcher met with all the teachers from the school and gave clear directions for the teachers in explaining to the students how their parents should complete the questionnaires. In this case, the survey process was called a *two-day survey turn around*. All the teachers distributed the questionnaires to the students and the students immediately were told when they saw their parents to ask them to complete the questionnaire without delay so that they could return the questionnaires by the next day. Two days were allowed to complete this process, which was found to be efficient rather than giving parents a greater length of time. The researcher also allowed an additional one week for any parents who were out of town or had extenuating circumstances in order to complete the survey. Teachers were also instructed to keep a list of all the students whose parents returned the questionnaires so that the researcher would know how many people and from which classes questionnaires were completed and to have a checks-and-balances system to ensure a credible process.

Undoubtedly, every researcher is faced with participants who do not complete the survey (step nine). Extenuating situations often occur to prevent a participant from responding in a timely fashion. For example, participants might be absent, on vacation, or preoccupied with other activities and the researcher needs to follow up with these people. It is important to allow a reasonable amount of time to follow up with nonrespondents to obtain the highest rate of return. The researcher needs to make a professional judgement, if the rate of return appears to be too low, of whether to continue the study. Given that every situation is different, which impacts the rate of return, it might be necessary to have a total of three or four follow-up survey administrations in order to obtain an acceptable return. The researcher needs to develop a follow-up letter that will be different than the initial cover letter. The follow-up letter contains the similar information, but is worded differently in order to produce a better return. If the same letter is sent, the respondents might still fail to complete the questionnaire. The follow-up letter could have more personal appeal or attractiveness than the initial letter in order to achieve higher effectiveness. In some cases, if the researcher knows the respondents, he or she could call them personally in order to encourage them to participate in the process. Also, the use of postcards and e-mail can be a helpful reminder in improving the rate of return.

Another important concern for the researcher is administering a survey to participants when the group is too small. For example, a consultant might be administering a survey to all the teachers within a school and the analysis might be calculated based upon departments If a department has a small number of teachers, anonymity will be compromised. One general rule in conducting organizational surveys is that a department should have at least five members in order to ensure a minimum degree of anonymity. Otherwise, if the group is too small, the group might need to be combined with another group.

Step ten consists of *analyzing the data* from the questionnaires. Although methods to analyze data is covered in a later chapter, special features can be employed in designing and administering the questionnaire that will make later analysis easier (Figure 3.29). This survey consists of a typical organizational survey in which teachers are asked to give their opinions regarding their school. The survey is broken down into three groups

---

Name of School:_____

Directions: Please indicate your group, then answer the following questions.

Group #1: Grades 1-3   Group #2: Grades 4-5   Group #3: Grades 6-7

To what extent do you agree or disagree with the each statement?

1. School policies such as discipline and attendance are clearly stated and are fair.

1	2	3	4	5
Strongly Agree	Agree	Undecided	Disagree	Strongly Disagree

2. School policies and procedures are administered fairly and consistently enforced.

1	2	3	4	5
Strongly Agree	Agree	Undecided	Disagree	Strongly Disagree

3. I believe we are kept well informed on matters that effect us.

1	2	3	4	5
Strongly Agree	Agree	Undecided	Disagree	Strongly Disagree

4. Teachers' concerns are listened to and acted upon by administration.

1	2	3	4	5
Strongly Agree	Agree	Undecided	Disagree	Strongly Disagree

5. I believe students feel safe and are respected.

1	2	3	4	5
Strongly Agree	Agree	Undecided	Disagree	Strongly Disagree

6. Our school climate promotes student self-esteem and involvement.

1	2	3	4	5
Strongly Agree	Agree	Undecided	Disagree	Strongly Disagree

7. Teachers utilize effective instructional techniques.

1	2	3	4	5
Strongly Agree	Agree	Undecided	Disagree	Strongly Disagree

8. Teachers utilize adequate instructional resources.

1	2	3	4	5
Strongly Agree	Agree	Undecided	Disagree	Strongly Disagree

9. I feel the curriculum at our school is effective.

1	2	3	4	5
Strongly Agree	Agree	Undecided	Disagree	Strongly Disagree

10. I believe students are receiving a quality education at our school.

1	2	3	4	5
Strongly Agree	Agree	Undecided	Disagree	Strongly Disagree

Figure 3.29. Organizational Survey

11. I believe morale is high among teachers at our school.

1	2	3	4	5
Strongly Agree	Agree	Undecided	Disagree	Strongly Disagree

12. I believe interpersonal relations among the teachers are good.

1	2	3	4	5
Strongly Agree	Agree	Undecided	Disagree	Strongly Disagree

13. There is good parent and community involvement at our school.

1	2	3	4	5
Strongly Agree	Agree	Undecided	Disagree	Strongly Disagree

14. I believe the parents and community respect and support our school.

1	2	3	4	5
Strongly Agree	Agree	Undecided	Disagree	Strongly Disagree

15. I believe that teachers carry their fair share of the workload.

1	2	3	4	5
Strongly Agree	Agree	Undecided	Disagree	Strongly Disagree

16. Teachers are willing to volunteer for extra responsibility beyond their regular duties.

1	2	3	4	5
Strongly Agree	Agree	Undecided	Disagree	Strongly Disagree

17. Our facilities are in good condition and are well maintained.

1	2	3	4	5
Strongly Agree	Agree	Undecided	Disagree	Strongly Disagree

18. Teachers freely give assistance to each other in getting work done.

1	2	3	4	5
Strongly Agree	Agree	Undecided	Disagree	Strongly Disagree

19. Faculty meetings are sufficient and regularly held.

1	2	3	4	5
Strongly Agree	Agree	Undecided	Disagree	Strongly Disagree

20. The bussing operates efficiently at our school.

1	2	3	4	5
Strongly Agree	Agree	Undecided	Disagree	Strongly Disagree

Figure 3.29.   Organizational Survey (continued)

according to grade level. The statements have been designed to reflect the organizational issues in the school. A five-point Likert scale is used to ask the participants their extent of agreement with each statement.

The statements in this organizational survey have also been categorized by dimensions (Figure 3.30) For example, the first two statements refer to the topic of policies. Therefore, dimension number one is labeled "policies." The third and fourth questions pertain to the topic of communications. The fifth and sixth questions pertain to "student-centered learning." The other dimensions are instruction and resources, curriculum, organizational climate, etc.

	Dimension	Correlating Survey Questions
Dimension #1:	Policies	Questions #1–2
Dimension #2:	Communications	Questions #3–4
Dimension #3:	Student-centered learning	Questions #5–6
Dimension #4:	Instruction and resources	Questions #6–8
Dimension #5:	Curriculum	Questions #9–10
Dimension #6:	Organizational climate	Questions #11–12
Dimension #7:	Parent and community involvement	Questions #13–14
Dimension #8:	Work performance	Questions #15–16
Dimension #9:	Miscellaneous	Questions #17–20

Figure 3.30. Dimensions of the Organizational Survey

Constructing the survey in this manner will assist the researcher when he or she completes an analysis of the results. In analyzing the results, the researcher will be able to make an opinion regarding each of these dimensions, based on the respondents' degree of favorableness to each of these statements. Also, organizational surveys generally contain open-ended questions at the end of the questionnaire (Figure 3.31). These questions can help the action researcher gain additional information on the organization.

Step eleven consists of *conducting the feedback session*. Given that action research is a collaborative process that is concerned with solving educational problems and making school improvements, this step allows the participants to maintain involvement in the process. However, the feedback session is considered to be an optional step because it is possible that the participants do not need to be given the results. Generally, during the feedback session, the participants ask questions and learn about the results of the survey, but do not actually develop action plans until a later time. The feedback session is considered an opportunity for clarification. It generally does not allow sufficient time to allow participants to develop an action plan.

▸ Please describe the things you like best about your school.
▸ Please describe the things you like least about your school.
▸ Please write ideas for making improvements at your school.

Figure 3.31. Examples of Open-ended Questions

In some instances, even in action research, a feedback session might not be sensible or practical. For example, if a teacher administers a survey to his or her students, it might not be necessary to inform the students of the results. The results might be useful for the teacher in making action plans if the teacher feels that the results of the survey are too sensitive or simply not useful for them. In most cases, if a researcher asks respondents to participate in a survey, they should have a right to know the results. For example, if a principal administers an organizational survey to all of his or her teachers, then it would seem logical that the teachers would get a copy of the results and would be involved in the development of action plans to address the issues.

A general rule in conducting an organizational survey is that teachers should not be asked questions if the administrator does not intend to do anything about the issues. The researcher should also be careful not to raise false hopes or expectations which will discourage them from participating in future surveys. Likewise, the same argument can be made conerning students in a classroom. If a teacher asks the students to complete a survey, then most likely, unless there is sensitive information, the results should be shared with the students.

The *development of action plans* to address the issues in a survey is step twelve. This step is covered in more detail in chapter 5. However, basic to the action research process is the development of action plans to address the issues and ultimately make school improvements. This process generally works best when done in a collaborative effort involving all participants. For example, if a survey was administered to parents of students, it might be wise to give the results of the survey to the parents and ask them to become part of the process of developing action plans.

The last step of the survey process involves *follow up* (step 14). Several approaches are used to follow up on assessing the results of the actions. A survey can be re-administered to assess the effectiveness of the actions or follow up interviews can be conducted, etc. For example, if an organization survey was administered to all the teachers, the researcher could follow up with the teachers at a six-month interval by holding department meetings to openly discuss the effectiveness of the survey process and the results of the actions that were implemented. Although the researcher might find it most useful to re-administer the same survey, sometimes the availability of resources, such as time and money, can prevent administering the survey.

Individual Surveys Although the survey is generally administered to groups of people, there are special situations in which a survey can be administered to an individual. For example, if the principal is experiencing performance problems with a teacher, he or she could conduct a coaching session with the teacher using the action research process. If the teacher is having difficulty in managing discipline, the principal could begin the coaching session by identifying the problem and then collecting data by asking the teacher to complete a discipline styles inventory. By completing the survey instrument, the teacher can assess his or her discipline style, which can be used as a basis of discussion for developing actions to improve the teacher's performance. Through this diagnostic process, it might be identified that the teacher is using a discipline style that is too "supporting" and he or she might need to develop a more "assertive" disciplinary style. The results of using an individual survey, followed up with discussion of the responses and development of action plans, can be a viable process when working with an individual.

Another example of administering a survey to an individual is when a teacher is experiencing a student who is having difficulty listening to the teacher and to fellow classmates. The teacher, like the principal, could begin by identifying the listening problem and then collecting data by asking the student to complete a listening profile. In this instrument, the student rates his or her ability to listen, based on different factors, which can then be discussed by the teacher and student. Action plans can then be made to help address the issues.

Two-way Surveys

The definition of a two-way survey means that the questionnaire is administered to a group of respondents, an analysis is made, and the results are then reviewed with the respondents. The meeting is generally called a *feedback session,* where the respondents gain clarification as to the results of their collective responses. A two-way survey is one of the more popular methods of action research because it allows the participants to take an active role in understanding the group's responses and developing action plans to address the issues. Unlike action research, many surveys do not allow for this two-way process to take place with the respondents. Quite often in survey research, data is gathered from the respondents, but they are never given the results of the survey or are actively involved in the study. This is one of the unique features of action research because it promotes active involvement of the participants in solving educational problems. Therefore, the design and administration of a survey, when used in action research, should generally be done with this two-way process.

In action research, surveys are designed with open-ended questions as well as closed-ended statements. The open-ended statements allow for the respondents to give their honest and candid responses in a narrative form (Figure 3.31).

One-way Surveys

Although most surveys, when used in the action research process, are designed as a two-way process, the one-way survey is sometimes used. The one-way survey is administered to respondents and the data is collected and analyzed and the respondents are never involved in actually obtaining the results of the survey or actively involved in developing action plans to address the issues. For example, the teacher might be interested in conducting an action research study in which he or she desires to assess the opinions of parents regarding student study habits. After the parents complete this one-way survey, the teacher analyzes responses and then, based on this information, develops action plans to improve the study habits of students without the parents ever obtaining the results of the survey. Although this approach is acceptable in action research, the researcher needs to make a decision whether a two-way process would be more beneficial or if the one-way process is more efficient. Regardless of whether the survey is a one-way or two-way process, the questionnaire could include both closed-ended and open-ended questions.

ASSESSING

Assessing is another technique used in collecting data in action research. Assessing involves the evaluation of individuals' work by examining tests, portfolios, records, and through the direct observation of individual and group skills and behaviors. Assessing student performance can be more practical than observing, interviewing, or surveying when the data exists or assessment provides more practical and richer information for the action research study.

Portfolios

The word "portfolio" is derived from the Latin term "portare," meaning leafs or sheets of paper. The *American Dictionary* describes a portfolio as "a portable case for holding loose sheets of paper, drawings, and the like." The portfolio has similar meaning for educators. The portfolio can be defined as a collection of a student's work, such as drawings, writings, papers, projects, and personal reflections, and related materials that can be used to judge his or her performance. The portfolio can be developed by the student in collaboration with his or her teachers. The portfolio contents can be contained in a three-ring binder, box, or suitable container. The key for developing a portfolio should be based upon the criteria of performance.

The idea of the portfolio, as used in action research, allows the researcher the opportunity to assess the student's work, which can give valuable information in identifying problems in the student's performance and assisting in developing actions for improvements. Roger Farr (1994) describes several advantages for portfolio assessment, such as "they encourage and develop self-assessment, provide varied and broad perspectives, integrate reading and writing with thinking, and should be authentic" (p. 5). With this in mind, portfolios can provide a convenient method for the researcher in evaluating a student's work, especially over a long-term period. An advantage of using the portfolio for assessment versus tests in action research is that they often give a better reflection of the student's overall performance. Examples of artifacts that can be contained in the student portfolio include: performance tests, papers, teacher observations, anecdotal notes, meetings with parents, personal student logs, and homework materials (Figure 3.32).

For example, if a teacher is experiencing a problem with a student who has shown a sudden decrease in reading performance, the teacher could make an assessment of the student's portfolio to gain insight as to the possible root cause of the problem. By reading the portfolio, the teacher

▶ Contains student's interests and ideas
▶ Includes other teachers' observations and anecdotal notes
▶ Contains meeting notes from meetings with parents
▶ Contains self-reflection notes
▶ Includes student's attitude toward work
▶ Provides introspective materials
▶ Contains actual student drawings and other materials
▶ Contains comments from conferences
▶ Contains writings and actual projects
▶ Contains photographs, and video and audio recordings of student work

Figure 3.32.   Advantages of Portfolio Assessment

might identify that the student, through his or her self-reflections, has been experiencing increased conflict at home. Also, the researcher might identify through a teacher's checklist that the student has not been completing reading homework assignments. Based upon a review of these materials, the researcher might surmise from the increased conflict and lack of reading homework that the student's home environment could be causing the decrease in reading performance. A follow-up interview with the student might confirm the researcher's assessment of the portfolio in making a diagnosis for the problem. Roger Farr supports the benefit of using the portfolio as an assessment by stating, "That kind of analysis is surely a more dependable indicator that counting responses to multiple-choice test items. The portfolio collection should clearly indicate the questions you and the student can consider about why comprehension may have been limited" (p. 245).

Testing

Action research is more practical than qualitative and quantitative research designs mainly because it takes less time for data collection and analysis. Most educators simply do not have the time to conduct extensive research. Likewise, testing is one of the more convenient methods of data collection. Because teachers commonly administer tests, it is convenient for them to analyze this data outside of the classroom. Testing is often a normal part of the teacher's job and the use of this data-collection technique can be more easily performed as long as it is appropriate for the given action research study. Figure 3.33 lists some examples of types of tests that can be used in action research.

Test: Subject matter tests
➡ *Description:* Teacher-constructed tests that measure student performance on classroom activities.

Test: Achievement tests
➡ *Description:* Standardized tests constructed by state or professional agencies.

Test: Aptitude tests
➡ *Description:* Professional tests that are often used for predictive measures of students' intelligence or ability.

Test: Intelligence tests
➡ *Description:* Professional tests administered to measure general intellectual abilities.

Test: Special tests
➡ *Description:* Tests that measure personality, values, interests, and other diagnostic measures.

Figure 3.33. Examples of Performance Tests

The use of *subject matter tests* as a normal activity for teaching is one of the more convenient methods of testing in action research. These tests, which are generally constructed by the teacher, can be used to assess student performance on such topics as reading, writing, mathematics, science, and language arts. For example, a teacher might use an intervention such as a new reading technique with the hopes of improving student reading comprehension. The teacher could then administer the regular test to the students and then compare the difference between the students' test performance as measured by the test for the students who participated in the new reading technique versus those students who were in the traditional reading program. Given that the teacher would be administering the test any way, an examination of these tests would be an easy way to note if there are differences between the classes based upon the reading techniques.

One concern with action research is the lack of validity and reliability of the tests. The term *validity* is defined as: "does the test truly measure what it purports to measure." *Reliability* refers to "the ability of the test to accurately measure consistently over time." Although the use of these tests might not have expert validity and reliability, they can still be useful in making assessments in action research.

The use of *standardized tests* can also be a useful and efficient way to test students. Most school districts utilize some form of a state or professional standardized test to measure student performance. An examination of the results of these tests by students can give the teacher valuable information in collecting data on students. For example, if an administrator is conducting an action research study in an attempt to measure the performance of an entire school, the use of standardized tests could help him or her in making this assessment.

The use of *aptitude tests* and other special tests are other methods available for student assessment by the action researcher. For example, if a teacher is attempting to conduct an action research study in improving the self-esteem of students, the use of a special test that measures self-esteem could be valuable in making this assessment. Teachers should be careful when conducting action research to ensure than no harm comes to any of the students, especially when using personality inventories. Use of these types of tests, such as Minnesota Multiphasic Personality Inventory (MMPI) and other personality diagnostic tests should only be administered by trained professionals. Some examples of typical achievement tests include the California Achievement Test, the Stanford Achievement Test, the Iowa Test of Basic Skills, and the Metropolitan Achievement Test. Examples of other specialized tests include the California Psychological Inventory, Stanford Benet Intelligence Test, Wechsler Intelligence Test, Strong-Campbell Interest Inventory, Work Values Inventory, Survey of School Attitudes, and the Tennessee Self-Concept Scale.

There are basically two types of standardized tests: norm-referenced instruments and criterion-referenced instruments. Norm-referenced tests compare a student's score against the scores of a known group, such as a district, state, or nation. These tests can be valuable in comparing students' scores with other students. Criterion-referenced tests measure a student's performance based upon a pre-established standard of performance as determined by experts. These tests are especially helpful in estimating a student's level of performance and identifying deficiencies based upon pre-established criteria. For example, a criterion-referenced test might indicate that a student "spelled nine of ten words correctly," or "correctly solved eight of ten math problems." A norm-referenced test, on the other hand, would indicate the student's score as compared to a known group (such as "scored in the 80th percentile nationwide" or "scored in the top ten percent, as compared to students statewide"). Both types of tests can be useful in making assessments in action research.

Records

Action researchers should never overlook the possibility of using student records to help collect data. There are many sources for student records, such as the student's permanent file, past teacher records, disciplinary dean's records, and records of counselors and other special services. These files contain valuable information in which the action researcher can gain insight in collecting data, such as the student's past attitudes, values, emotional and behavioral disorders, academic abilities, and past home environment characteristics. For example, a teacher might conduct an action research study to measure the impact of single parent versus two parent families on student behavior or achievement. The use of these records could provide a valuable source of data for the researcher.

PROCESSING

Processing is a method of data collection that is especially useful for analyzing situations and learning environments. The objective of using processing techniques is to facilitate individual or group structured sessions to brainstorm causes of problems that serve as a basis for decision

Processing Technique: Team Building
➡ *Description:* A structured session where team members exchange ideas, brainstorm causes for problems, and make action plans for improvement.
Processing Technique: Brainstorming
➡ *Description:* A structured approach whereby individuals meet to collectively generate possible causes for problems and ideas for solutions.
Processing Technique: Story Boarding
➡ *Description:* A problem-solving process whereby groups develop visual displays to diagram possible causes and solutions to problems.
Processing Technique: Cause and Effect Diagram
➡ *Description:* To portray, using a fishbone diagram, potential causes and effects of a problem.
Processing Technique: Force-Field Analysis
➡ *Description:* The "field theory" technique used to identify the hindering and supporting elements of a problem, which can be used for change and decision making.
Figure 3.34. Examples of Processing Techniques for Data Assessment

making. The use of processing techniques is an outgrowth from the *Total Quality Management initiative (TQM)*. TQM is a philosophy that embraces the idea of making continuous improvements to meet or exceed customer expectations. The concepts of TQM rely heavily upon the use of teamwork, problem-solving techniques, quality improvement, innovation and creativity, benchmarking, and customer satisfaction, which are all common elements of action research (Camp, 1989). Several processing techniques can be used in action research (Figure 3.34).

The *team building* session is a processing technique that can be helpful when a researcher desires to identify problems that affect an intact team. For example, a department chairperson who is experiencing problems within his or her department could assemble his or her staff and conduct a team building session. In this session, the team members identify all the possible causes of problems that negatively affect the department's performance. Some of these possible causes include unclear goals, role incongruency, poor leadership, poor accountability, inadequate resources, or poor time management. These issues are often generated by a facilitator who lists all the possible issues freely identified by the members of the team. The group would then, by consensus, prioritize the issues that are most in need of improvement. Action plans are then developed to address the issues.

The *brainstorming* technique is another processing technique, and is similar to team building, but does not require an intact team. Brainstorming involves the pre-generation of ideas that cause problems. For example, a teacher could work with his or her colleagues in brainstorming a list of all the possible reasons for poor student achievement. During this free-wheeling session, no criticism is allowed. The teacher acts as a facilitator and records all of the ideas on a flip chart or chalkboard, which are then later analyzed. Action plans are then made to address the issues.

Story Boarding

The story boarding technique is a processing technique that is useful in producing a visual picture of processes and procedures. This technique was originally credited to Walt Disney in the early 1900s when he pinned completed drawings in sequence on studio walls so that the production crew could better visualize the animated story. The process of

Topic

Statement of the problem

Bussing Schedule	Homeroom Period	1st period class	2nd period class	3rd period class	4th period class	lunch period	5th period class	6th period class	7th period class
problem issue	problem issue	problem issue	problem issue	problem issue	problem issue	problem issue	problem issue	problem issue	problem issue
problem issue #2	problem issue #2	problem issue #2	problem issue #2	problem issue #2	problem issue #2	problem issue #2	problem issue #2	problem issue #2	problem issue #2
problem issue #3	problem issue #3	problem issue #3	problem issue #3	problem issue #3	problem issue #3	problem issue #3	problem issue #3	problem issue #3	problem issue #3
problem issue #4	problem issue #4	problem issue #4	problem issue #4	problem issue #4	problem issue #4	problem issue #4	problem issue #4	problem issue #4	problem issue #4

Figure 3.35. Story Boarding Process

story boarding can be useful to the action researcher. For example, a school administrator can identify a problem of excessive tardiness among the students. He or she could assemble a group of teachers to develop the sequence of activities as students progress to classes throughout the day (Figure 3.35).

The story boarding process begins with identifying the topic (e.g., excessive tardiness). Then, the entire sequence of events for the students' day are outlined using *headers* such as: bus schedule, homeroom, first period, second period, etc. Underneath each header, the teachers, through use of cards which are pinned to a wall, list different situations which cause student tardiness for each event. When completed, the group can view the story board, identify problems, and then develop actions to address the issues.

The *cause and effect diagram* is a processing method that is especially useful in identifying technical problems. This technique, often called the *fishbone diagram*, provides a pictorial method of breaking down central problems in an understandable diagram. The objective of this fishbone diagram is to list the *effect* and *causes* of a problem that can then later be used to make decisions for improvement (Figure 3.36). For example, an administrator could identify the effect as "poor student academic achievement." The administrator then could brainstorm with a group of teachers to identify the major categories of causes that may be contributing to the poor student achievement. These might consist of poor teaching, instructional methods, curriculum, and school climate. Each of these categories would represent the branches of the diagram (i.e., fishbone arrangement). The group would then brainstorm specific causes for each of the major categories. For example, under the category of "school

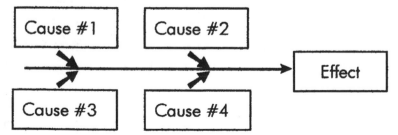

Figure 3.36.   Example of Cause and Effect Diagram

culture," possible causes might include poor teacher morale, excessive discipline incidents, unsafe school, poor facilities, and presence of gangs. Under the category of "teaching," possible causes might include inexperienced teachers, apathy, low motivation, poor teaching skills, and poor placement of teachers. The category called "instruction" could include lack of innovative instruction, outdated instructional techniques, poor facilities for instruction, and inadequate instructional resources. The last major category, "curriculum," might include out-dated instructional materials, poor curricular resources, inadequate resource guides, and insufficient curriculum. The number of major categories and their subcauses can vary, depending on the statement of the problem.

The *force-field analysis*, although not specifically designed as a problem-solving technique, can be an effective processing technique for collecting data. This technique, developed by Kurt Lewin (1943), was originally designed as a group process for initiating change. The process involves identifying the *driving forces* (factors that promote change) and *restraining forces* (factors that hinder change). The result of these counter forces creates a polarization that prevents change from occurring (Figure 3.37).

Lewin stated that in order to create change, either the restraining forces must be reduced, the driving forces strengthened, or a combination of both. This technique can be useful for the action researcher in identifying the restraining forces (causes of problems) that hinder effective change. For example, if a teacher is conducting an action research study with the objective of improving reading skills, the force-field analysis technique could be used. The teacher could identify all the

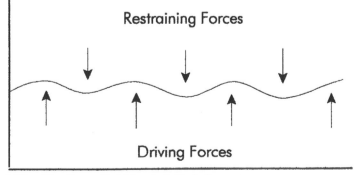

Figure 3.37. The Force-Field Analysis Technique

restraining forces that are hindering effective reading achievement, such as poor reading material, lack of parental support, low student motivation, inadequate reading resources, and poor reading instructional techniques. The driving forces could also be identified, such as the need to improve test scores, state mandates for reading improvements, and school district board policies. The teacher could use this technique as either an individual or group problem-solving process.

DATA ANALYSIS
AND INTERPRETATION

THREATS TO VALIDITY

Before an action researcher begins to analyze data, he or she must understand the terms *validity* and *threats to validity*. Validity refers to the extent to which the data is accurate and useful. For example, if an action researcher administers a survey to assess the opinions of students' knowledge of science, he or she needs to validate that the survey actually measures science content. In other words, does the survey actually accomplish what it is intended to measure? Therefore, any factors that negatively impact on the validity of the data can be called *threats to validity*. Guarding against threats to validity are especially important in quantitative research, given the need for preciseness, and are generally harder to control in action research. Campbell Stanley first established several threats to validity in 1963 (Figure 4.1).

History

The concept of *history* can have a negative effect upon data collection. This concept refers to the fact that many factors can affect the nature of data if collected at different points in time. Few things in life remain

Threat: History
➡ *Working Definition:* Effects on data when collected at different points in time.

Threat: Maturation
➡ *Working Definition:* Physical, mental, or psychological development of people that affect the data collection.

Threat: Instrumentation
➡ *Working Definition:* The negative effects of the method used to collect data.

Threat: Attrition
➡ *Working Definition:* The loss of participants during the study.

Threat: Testing
➡ *Working Definition:* The negative effects of a pretest on data collection.

Threat: Differential Selection
➡ *Working Definition:* The negative effects of comparing dissimilar groups.

Threat: Hawthorne Effect
➡ *Working Definition:* Attention given to people that motivates them to perform better.

Threat: Researcher Bias
➡ *Working Definition:* The researcher's unconscious or conscious preference that affects the outcome of a study.

Threat: Contamination
➡ *Working Definition:* Any factors that negatively impact on the natural setting of the study.

Figure 4.1.   Examples of Threats to Validity

constant. For example, if a researcher administers an attitude survey to teachers, he or she most likely will obtain different types of data, depending upon which point in time during the school year it is administered. If it is administered during mid-year, the results will be different than if it is administered at year-end, just prior to summer vacation. Teachers are most likely to have more negative attitudes at the end of the school year than at mid-year. Likewise, if an action researcher is collecting data over an extended period of time, the data could vary simply because changes occurred during this process. Any number of factors can affect the data, such as world events, economic crises, policy changes, traumatic events, etc. The action researcher should be careful to identify any factors that might impact the validity of the data and strive to obtain data under natural conditions.

Maturation

Maturation refers to the physical, mental, or psychological changes that occurs in the participants. When researching elementary students, this factor is especially important because students at this age group are maturing at a quicker pace than in adulthood. For example, if a researcher is collecting data in an attempt to observe the impact of a new teaching strategy, the positive gains that are obtained might be explained by the fact that the students matured and not that the teaching strategy was more effective. In experimental research, the researcher would include a control group, which could help control for this effect because it is used in comparing the results between this control group and the treatment group. In action research, the researcher should try and control for maturation by also using a control group or observing any changes in development.

Instrumentation

The term *instrumentation* refers to the method in which data is collected (e.g., survey, observation, or interviews). Therefore, the use of instrumentation, in itself, can impact the validity of the data being collected. For example, if a researcher is using the interview technique, it is possible that he or she might obtain more favorable responses simply because the respondent feels favorable toward the interviewer. Likewise, if the respondent feels unfavorable toward the interviewer, more negative responses might be obtained. The use of instrumentation might have a negative effect if the action researcher selects the wrong type of instrument for collecting data. It is possible that a researcher might, under certain situations, obtain more favorable responses during the interview process than if he or she were to use a questionnaire. Respondents are less likely to give critical opinions than if given complete anonymity through the use of a questionnaire.

Attrition

The term *attrition* refers to the loss of participants during the data-collection process. For example, if an action researcher is collecting data over an extended period of time and there are several student absences, the data will be effected. The action researcher must always use common sense to ensure that there is a minimum loss of participants during data collection. For example, an action research technique is when the researcher administers a survey to a group of students. If, during the survey administration, several students are absent, the researcher needs to follow up with the absent students and obtain their responses to acquire maximum participation. Although there is no absolute rule for how many participants a researcher must have from a known sample population, the researcher must attempt to obtain as many as possible; otherwise, the researcher should not continue with the study.

Testing

A common practice in action research is when the researcher administers a pretest, implements an action, and then administers a post-test. If both the pre- and post-tests are similar, the students might have learned enough from the pretest to show improvement on the post-test. This improvement might have nothing to do with the action administered, but rather simply because the students became "test wise." To guard against this potential problem, an action researcher might eliminate the pretest, use different tests, or make sure sufficient amount of time has lapsed before administering the post-test.

Differential Selection

The term *differential selection* refers to the fact that two groups can be dissimilar and therefore, the results can vary. For example, if a teacher administers action to one of two classes and then collects data on both classes for comparison, any differences can be explained because the two classes were different in the first place and not that the action was effective. In these types of cases, the action researcher needs to be sure that the two classes are similar in such characteristics as age, academic ability, gender, and behavior.

Hawthorne Effect

The *Hawthorne Effect* refers to the fact that when people are given attention, such as through participation in an action research study, they tend to be motivated to perform better. For example, if an action researcher is actually videotaping a group of students and they are aware of the recording, their behavior will probably be more positive than without the videotaping. Therefore, when conducting action research, the researcher must attempt to minimize the participants' awareness that they are participating in a study and attempt to maintain a natural environment.

Researcher Bias

The term *researcher bias* indicates the unconscious or conscious preference for a positive or negative outcome of the study. For example, if a researcher is administering an action and hopes that the result will be effective, he or she might tend to unconsciously slant the results more positive. Although this bias can be intentional or unintentional, the results negatively affect that quality of the data collected and the outcome. Therefore, the researcher must maintain high standards of ethics and integrity and always try to be neutral and objective when collecting data.

Contamination

The term *contamination* refers to any factors that negatively impact on the natural setting or in the actual collecting of data. Many factors might contaminate data collection, such as unexpected interruptions, use of video or audio recordings, poor instruments, or use of untrained researchers.

In experimental research, threats to validity are often controlled by using a control group to compare against a treatment group. In action research, a control group is not always used. Therefore, action research is more prone to experiencing threats to validity. The action researcher can try and control for threats to validity by recognizing them and trying to guard against them through observation and a little common sense. In medicine, a common saying is that medicine is "more of an art than a science." This statement refers to the fact the physicians often need to use their best clinical judgement and common sense in treating patients versus always adhering to pre-established medical protocol. Likewise, action researchers must use their clinical ability and common sense to guard against obvious threats to validity to ensure that the research is of the highest quality.

USING DESCRIPTIVE STATISTICS

The term *descriptive statistics* refers to the use of visual graphics, charts, diagrams, and basic mathematics to describe data. The use of descriptive statistics is the most common method of analyzing and displaying action research information. Other methods of statistical analysis, such as tests of significance, are seldom used with action research and are reserved for quantitative research.

Measures of Central Tendency

The use of *central tendency*, a common analysis technique used in action research, is a method to describe a set of data that is the "average" or "middle" score. This calculation is commonly used to compare the differences of the individual scores from the group. It is often called the "central point," around which data from the group are distributed. The three common measures of central tendency are the *mean, median*, and *mode* (Figure 4.2). The mean is the arithmetic average of the scores. The median represents the middle score of a set of scores, and the mode represents the most frequent score of a set of scores.

Mean = 79	Median = 80	Mode = 90

40	50	60	65	70	75	80	85	90	90	100	110	115

Mean	Median	Mode
The arithmetic average of the scores	The middle score of the set of scores	The most frequent score of the set of scores

Figure 4.2.   **Measures of Central Tendency for a Set of Data**

For example, if a teacher distributes a test and desires to calculate the average of the scores, he or she often calculates the mean average as a representative midpoint. To calculate the mean, add the total scores and divide this number by the number of scores. The median is commonly used to accurately depict a midpoint of a set of scores when the distribution of the scores are very low or high. The term *median* comes from the Latin word "middle." The median is often used to report information, such as teacher salaries, family income, or the value of residential homes. The median would be more useful than using the mean because it often represents the numerical center of the set of data, especially when the scores significantly vary. For example, many small towns typically have people with average salaries but often include one millionaire. Calculating the mean would not adequately represent the income of the families in this small town. However, the median would better represent this numerical midpoint because it would take into account the extreme income of the millionaire.

To calculate the median score, simply arrange the scores in order and then select the middle score from the group. Another method of calculating a median for ungrouped data is to add the total number of scores plus one and divide by two, which gives the numeric position. Then, arrange the scores in order and starting from the bottom, count each score until the numeric measure is obtained. This midpoint will be the median. If the position includes a half measure, then find the midpoint of the distance between the two whole numbers to indicate the median. For example, if the median is between 15 and 16, then the half median score is 15.5.

The mode is the most frequent score of a set of scores and is probably the least reliable of the measures of central tendency. In reality, the mode tends to represent the most common score, as opposed to a given mid-point of a set of scores. Although it has limited value, it does allow a researcher to identify a common score from a group, which can gain insight in making interpretations. For example, if most students on a test incorrectly answered a particular test item (i.e., the most frequently missed question), the teacher could then examine this test item for the possibility of being a poor question. The teacher then might, upon examination, revise the question.

It is important that the action researcher select the best measure of tendency when making analysis and interpretation. Likewise, the action researcher must use common sense in realizing that the use of measurers of central tendency is a form of statistics and that sometimes no measure of central tendency will adequately describe a set of data. For example, consider a situation in which five cars are sitting in a parking lot. The first two cars are total junk and have a total value of $50.00 each. The third car is an old, beat-up vehicle with several mechanical problems and has a total value of $1,000.00. The fourth car is an economy car and has a total value of $10,000.00. The last car is a custom-made, high-performance, experimental vehicle and has a value of three million dollars. Which measure of central tendency might a researcher use to describe this set of data (i.e., the five cars in the parking lot)? If we were to select the mode, the answer would be $50.00. This, however, does little justice in describing the five cars, especially the fifth car. If we were to use the median, the answer would be $1,000.00. Although this adequately represents the third vehicle, it does little justice for the first two or last two cars. If we were to calculate the mean average, the answer would be $3,011,100.00 divided by five, which equals $602,220.00. This figure certainly does little justice for describing the first four vehicles, and certainly significantly underestimates the fifth vehicle. Therefore, this example illustrates that no measure of central tendency adequately represents this set of data because the scores have such extreme variance.

Measures of Variability

Although it is not important for the action researcher to understand inferential statistics, having a basic understanding of measures of variability can help the researcher when interpreting data. The *measure of variability* indicates a statistic that can describe the dispersion, or spread, of the scores. It is different from a measure of central tendency because, rather than representing a midpoint or an average score, it describes a measure of distance, relative to the set of scores. A use of a measure of variation is typically associated with distribution of data that forms a normal curve (Figure 4.3). Several terms are used to describe the normal curve, such as the bell-shaped curve, symmetrical curve, and the empirical curve. Some of the terms used to interpret the normal

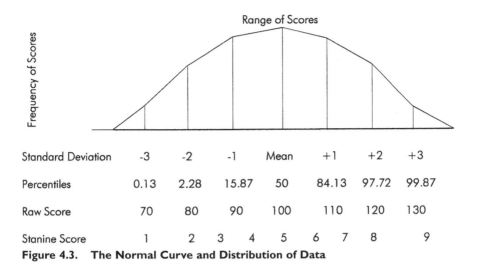

Standard Deviation	-3	-2	-1	Mean	+1	+2	+3
Percentiles	0.13	2.28	15.87	50	84.13	97.72	99.87
Raw Score	70	80	90	100	110	120	130
Stanine Score	1	2	3	4	5 6	7	8	9

Figure 4.3.   The Normal Curve and Distribution of Data

curve are: *the range, variance,* and *standard deviation*. The range represents the difference from the lowest to the highest score in the group. It is the measure of least reliability because its value can be affected by a single score that could extend significantly at the low or high end of the distribution. However, the range is still a good crude measure of checking the distribution of the scores.

The term *variance* refers to the measure of dispersion of the scores from the measure of central tendency (e.g., mean average). This *measure of variability* can be useful in helping to describe how much variance the scores have in relation to the average score. Standard deviation is the way of measuring the dispersion of the scores (i.e., variance). In the normal curve, approximately 68% of the scores will be contained in the area between plus one and minus one standard deviation from the mean. Approximately 95% of the scores will be contained in between plus and minus two standard deviations, and more than 99% will be included between plus and minus three standard deviation from the mean (Figure 4.3). For example, if a group of student raw scores were plotted on the normal curve, it might represent a range from 70–130. The score of seventy would indicate the lowest-performing student and the score of 130 would represent the highest-performing student. The mean average of all the students would be 100. Therefore, using the normal curve, approximately 68% of scores would be between 90 and 110.

Ninety-five percent of scores would exist between 80 and 120, and more than 99% of the scores would be contained between 70 and 130. Therefore, the use of standard deviation can be a valuable measure in portraying the distance of the scores away from the average score. Although the action researcher might not always find it necessary to calculate the standard deviation for a set of scores, he or she can use existing data in which the standard deviation is given, and having an understanding of this statistic can be useful in making interpretations.

The normal curve represents a distribution in which the mean, median, and mode are equal to each other. Therefore, the normal curve is perfectly symmetrical because both sides of the curve from the mean are identical. If a set of data does not form a symmetrical curve on one side and the two sides are unequal, the distribution is referred to as a *skewed distribution*. A skewed distribution indicates that the median and mean are different from each other and that the distribution is unequal. For example, if a teacher gave a very difficult test to a group of students and only a few performed well, the distribution would lack symmetry and would represent a *negative skewed* distribution. Likewise, if the teacher administered a test that was too easy, and most of the students scored high, the distribution would show a *positive skew*.

One of the more common uses of the normal curve and variability for the action researcher is interpreting state, national, and standardized tests. Teachers, when conducting action research, often rely upon state and national tests to extract data and make analyses. These tests generally include measures of central tendency and variability. Therefore, the need to understand these terms is important for the action researcher in making analysis and conclusions. For example, most standardized tests report the percentiles, and other standard scores, which are represented by Stanines, Z scores, and T scores. These standard scores are used so that students' performance on tests can be interpreted nationwide. For example, the Stanine score includes the numbers from one through nine, with five being the average. A Stanine of five represents the fifty percentile of a set of scores in a distribution. If a student were to score in the Stanine of nine, this would indicate that the student has scored exceptionally high, in the very top end of the distribution (i.e., commonly called the *tail*). Likewise, if a student scored with a Stanine one, this would indicate that the student performed very poorly and is in the lowest percentile of the distribution.

Consider an action research study in which the use of variability and measures of central tendency can be applied. For example, an action researcher conducts an organizational survey of all the teachers at a school in an effort to identify problems so that improvements can be later made. Assume that the first three questions of the survey are:

1. The school climate promotes student self-esteem.
2. Our concerns are listened to and acted upon by the administration.
3. School policies are clearly stated.

If the survey questionnaire included a standard Likert scale in which the respondents indicate their extend of agreement by circling a value between one and five (strongly agree, agree, undecided, disagree, and strongly disagree), after the survey has been administered, the action researcher would need to tally the responses. Descriptive statistics could be used to make this analysis. The action researcher could calculate the mean, standard deviation, and frequency for each of the responses to each of the items on the questionnaire (Figure 4.4).

Figure 4.4 illustrates a sample of this analysis. For example, question number one, which pertains to the extent of agreement for student self-esteem, indicates that the mean is a 2.79, standard deviation is 1.13, and the total cumulative percentage for the respondents who agreed with the question is 46.88%. A total of 35 respondents answered this question. Of the 35 teachers, only 17 responded favorably (46.88%). As an action researcher, this would be cause for concern. The action researcher would then make an analysis that less than half of the teachers were positive toward their school in providing a climate that promotes student self-esteem. Therefore, the action researcher would need to further investigate this question by talking with the teachers and gaining clarification of this problem.

Likewise, the second question indicates that only 35.29% of the teachers feel that their concerns are listened to and acted upon (mean equals 3.15). Given that less than half the teachers feel positive toward this item, the action researcher would also want to gain further clarification on this item. The third question indicates that more than 38.24% of the teachers are "undecided" regarding whether school policies are clearly stated. Moreover, only about 26.47% of the teachers were positive toward this item. In this case, the action researcher

Variable: Q1, The school climate promotes student self-esteem

				Cumulative		Cumulative
		Value	Frequency	frequency	Percent	percent
Strongly agree		1	2	2	6.25	6.25
Agree		2	13	15	40.63	46.88
Undecided		3	10	25	31.25	78.13
Disagree		4	5	30	15.63	93.75
Strongly disagree		5	2	32	6.25	100.00

Mean = 2.79 $S_D = 1.13$

Variable: Q2, Concerns are listened to and acted upon by the administration

Mean = 3.15 $S_D = 1.27$

				Cumulative		Cumulative
		Value	Frequency	frequency	Percent	percent
Strongly agree		1	2	2	5.88	5.88
Agree		2	10	12	29.41	35.29
Undecided		3	6	18	17.65	52.94
Disagree		4	9	27	26.47	79.41
Strongly disagree		5	7	34	20.59	100.00

Variable: Q3, School policies are clearly stated

Mean = 3.09 $S_D = 1.09$

				Cumulative		Cumulative
		Value	Frequency	frequency	Percent	percent
Strongly agree		1	4	4	11.75	11.76
Agree		2	5	9	14.71	26.47
Undecided		3	13	22	38.24	64.71
Disagree		4	10	32	29.41	94.12
Strongly disagree		5	2	34	5.88	100.00

Figure 4.4. · **Sample of Analysis of Survey Data**

might identify this item as a concern and gain further information about the issue.

As a rule, when interpreting data, an action researcher would identify an area in need of improvement as any item that the majority of respondents (e.g., approximately two-thirds of the respondents) did not rate positively. If an item were to be positively viewed by the majority of respondents (e.g., two-thirds of the participants or more), then the action researcher would indicate that this item is a strength. Although there is no absolute standard on which the action researcher makes his or her conclusions as to which items are considered a strength (i.e., positive item) or weakness (i.e., area of concern). A general guideline includes: if more than 50% disagree or strongly disagree with an item, the issue should be identified as a concern.

A common method of collecting data and making an analysis is through the use of observation. For example, a teacher could conduct an action research study by observing students' misbehavior in the classroom. The teacher might desire to identify the different types of disciplinary offenses. If a checklist were used to identify the disciplinary problems, several of the types of disciplinary offenses could be listed and the teacher could observe students and place a check for each incident of misbehavior (Figure 4.5).

After observing the students for a period of time (e.g., one week), the teacher could then tally up the marks (i.e., frequency or mode) and then identify the most frequent offenses. This approach could be very helpful in isolating a specific type of misbehavior so that the teacher could then develop an action plan to address the issue. This checklist could also be helpful in establishing a baseline of student

Directions: Mark an "x" for each time you observe the student misbehavior.

Student Misbehavior	Frequency	Total
Use of profanity	x	1
Defiance or disrespect	xxx	3
Talking without permission	xxxxx	5
Cheating or lying	x	1
Sleeping in class	xx	2
Apathy or low motivation	xxx	3
Harassing other students	xx	2
Tardiness or absenteeism	xxxx	4
Verbal fighting/arguing	xx	2
Physical fighting		0
Observation period: 1 week		Grand total: 23

Figure 4.5. Sample of Observation Frequency Form

behavior. Once the corrected action strategy is applied, the students can be observed again using the checklist. A comparison could then be made.

There are many uses for descriptive statistics in action research. Numerical information can assist the action researcher in providing quantifiable data in which to make analysis and interpretation. However, no amount of data can overcome the need for the action researcher to use common sense and inductive reasoning to ensure that the analysis and interpretation are meaningful for the action research study.

USING GRAPHS AND DIAGRAMS

The use of *graphs and diagrams* can be very helpful for the action researcher in displaying a visual picture of the data. The common expression, "A picture is worth a thousand words," is particularly useful for the action researcher in quickly observing data and making analysis. Moreover, the use of graphs can provide an easy method of presenting the data for the reader. For example, bar graphs are one of the

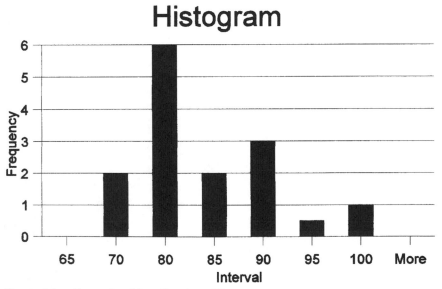

Figure 4.6.   **Example of Bar Graph or Histogram**

more commonly used methods to display survey data because they
provide a breakdown of the information into columns (Figure 4.6).
A bar graph, often called a *histogram*, can display data as a line graph,
or in a vertical or horizontal direction. The researcher needs to select
the best type of graph to display the data in the most easily understandable manner.

Pie charts are similar to the bar graphs except that a visual proportion
of the segments is given relative to the entire whole (Figure 4.7). For
example, if the researcher were conducting a survey of students and
wanted to present the responses indicating the percent of favorable responses among girls versus boys, a pie diagram could be used. In
essence, the pie chart gives a visual orientation by allowing the researcher to cut the pie into different sizes to illustrate different propor-
tions of responses. However, the researcher must be sure to not slice
the pie into too many pieces, otherwise the diagram will be cluttered
and hard to understand. For example, the pie chart could represent the
percentage of students who are deficient in reading per grade level.
The pie chart could indicate that the students in eighth grade are 50%
deficient in reading, seventh graders are 20% deficient, and sixth
graders represent 30% of the students that are deficient (Figure 4.7).

Grade Level Percentage

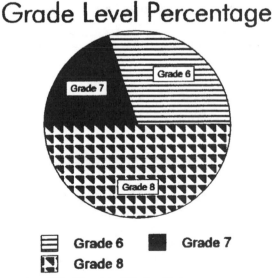

Figure 4.7.   **Example of Pie Chart to Display Data**

One of the more common computer software tools that can be used to create bar charts is Microsoft Excel. For example, if an action researcher wanted to construct a histogram for a set of math scores of students, the Excel program could be used. If the researcher had 14 students whose grades were 80, 87, 80, 85, 90, 70, 68, 78, 79, 80, 96, 84, 86, and 75, the data set could be converted into a histogram. The steps in performing this chart are:

Open Excel program
Enter the data set

3. Type (interval) in column E
   Column E, Row 2, type #65
   Row 3, type 70
   Row 4, type 80
   Row 5, type 85
   Row 6, type 90
   Row 7, type 95
   Row 8, type 100
   Click enter
   Click tools
   Click "data analysis" (Click tools "add ins" and check analysis tool pak VBA if needed)
   Click histogram and OK
   Input range equals A:A15
4. Bin range E1:E8
   Check labels
   Output range is G1
   Click OK
   The histogram for the display of this data should appear

The use of drawings can also be useful in displaying information visually. For example, if a teacher is conducting an action research study in an effort to identify factors that contribute to low student motivation, a *concept mapping* approach could be used (Figure 4.8). Through the use of a brainstorming session with a group of fellow teachers, the teacher could visually display all the factors that could be contributing

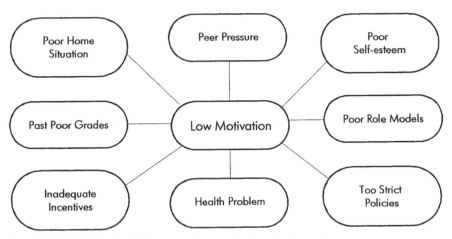

Figure 4.8. Example of Concept Map to Display Problem Issues

to low motivation. Once this concept map is displayed, the teacher could then conduct an action planning session to identify the most likely causes and suggest action plans for improvement.

WRITING NARRATIVE REPORTS

When conducting action research, the researcher will undoubtedly include a *narrative report*. The narrative report is a written description of the analysis of the data, which often includes references, measures of central tendency, and descriptive statistics. The report should be organized and succinct. The report should be written naturally, using short sentences and paragraphs, which can be most easily understood by the reader. Simple language should be used with proper formatting (e.g., use of headings, bold and italics, and a normal type size), which will help the reader understand the information. For example, the following is a sample of narrative report, providing the analysis and interpretation of a school survey.

A. Description of School
   The Smith Elementary School is located on 1st Avenue in New York City. There are about 500 children in grades Head Start through sixth grade. The student population reflects a diversity of backgrounds. Attendance is 96%, mobility is 39%, and truancy 2%. Ten

percent of students are at or above the national norms for reading and mathematics. The school, however, has been experiencing progressively low student test scores, higher discipline rates, and higher teacher attrition rates. Also, the principal has reported that morale among the teachers is low, especially within the past two years.

B. Description of Action Research Study

Therefore, an action research study was conducted, which included an organizational survey, to assess the teachers' opinions regarding the school in order to identify the issues that were contributing to the current problems. The survey was conducted in the beginning of the school year, was anonymous, and centered on group opinions and issues. The questionnaire consisted of a series of closed-ended questions and two open-ended questions asking the respondents to indicate what they "liked best about the school" and the "areas in need of improvement." The open-ended questions were typed and numbered for ease in reference and analysis. Although the responses were mainly summarized by the researcher based upon frequency (group strengths and concerns), the researcher also considered the "intensity" of the written responses (statements of serious concern). The report acted as a discussionary tool in gaining further clarification through feedback sessions and in developing action plans for improvement.

C. Survey Analysis: Strengths of the School

　　1. Student-Centered Learning

　　　More than eighty percent (80%) of the teachers believe the students at Smith School feel safe and are respected. Several written comments indicated that the teachers enjoy their students and that the students are well mannered, respectful, and responsible.

　　2. Quality of Education

　　　The quality of education the students are receiving is positively viewed by many of the teachers (85%). Also, overall, eighty-two percent (82%) of the teachers believe that the students are receiving good instruction. Several written comments supported this opinion.

D. Survey Analysis: Areas of Concern for the School

　　1. Leadership

　　　Without a doubt, leadership is a major concern of the teachers. One hundred percent (100%) of the teachers feel the principal is demeaning, condescending, and disruptive to the educational process. Several written comments indicated that the principal is disliked by the teachers and needs to be replaced.

2. Policies

There appears to be a major concern regarding school policies by the teachers. Only ten percent (10%) of the teachers feel the policies are fairly administered. Several written comments indicate that policies are: too strict and cause disciplinary problems among the students, contribute to low morale for both students and teachers, and create a negative climate within the school. Several written comments also indicated that poor policies are contributing to low test grades.

The narrative report generally combines the use of statistics, which are included in the written report and refer to supporting charts, diagrams, and tables. The length of the narrative report will depend upon the nature of the action research study. If a teacher is conducting an action research study in his or her classroom, he or she might not need to write an elaborate report. In this case, the teacher might be more concerned with making improvements than documenting the entire process. Documenting the process might be necessary if a teacher desires written evidence to support his or her good performance. However, when an extensive action research study is undertaken, a written report is generally necessary and the final report is often bound into a three-ring binder.

5

SOLVING PROBLEMS
AND TAKING ACTION

BARRIERS TO PROBLEM SOLVING

After an action researcher has analyzed the data, the next step is to identify the root cause(s) of the problem and initiate action. An important aspect to this problem-solving process is understanding some of the common barriers in problem solving (Figure 5.1).

Making False Comparisons

One potential barrier for the action researcher is *making false comparisons* when attempting to solve a problem. For example, the causes of disciplinary problems at one school might be entirely different than at another school. These differences (e.g., socioeconomics, teaching staff, environment, community, culture, and facilities) contribute to the students' behavior. If the researcher is trying to identify the root cause of a problem, he or she should be careful not to make a false comparison between schools (Tomal, 1999).

Failing to Identify the Cause

Another frequent barrier to problem solving is when the researcher attempts to solve a problem based upon a proposed solution without

- Making false comparisons
- Failing to identify the cause
- Failing to view the whole situation
- Falling into group polarization
- Failing to collaborate
- Failing to recognize hidden agendas
- Treating the symptom versus the cause of the problem

Figure 5.1.   Examples of Barriers to Problem Solving

first identifying the cause. For example, an administrator who is facing a disciplinary problem might state, "The solution to our problem is that we need more security officers" or "The solution to disciplinary problem is that we need more enforcement of policies by the administration." Attempting to solve a disciplinary problem based upon a proposed solution is futile without first isolating the actual cause.

Failing to View the Whole Situation

Another potential barrier is when the researcher fails to anticipate the widespread effects of an action upon the entire organization. For example, if an educator is working with a student who is having difficulty in learning and he or she feels that positive reinforcement is needed for the student, other students might become resentful. In this example, the educator could create additional problems by taking action to resolve one problem (i.e., failing to view the whole situation).

Falling into Group Polarization

The barrier of *falling into group polarization* is common when researchers are influenced by people (e.g., fellow colleagues, community members, or parents) to select a specific action. For example, if a teacher is working with a student who is having difficulty in learning, he or she might jump to the conclusion that the student is suffering from a learning disability, if influenced by the school psychologist or local school policy. The teacher might become "polarized" into thinking that all learning problems are associated with a learning disability.

Failing to Collaborate

When researchers *fail to collaborate* in solving problems, the results of the action plan will be compromised. The foundation of action research is based upon a collaborative effort in solving problems. Action researchers should always attempt to involve other people, especially the subjects of the study, when solving a problem. Groups of people generally make better decisions than individuals. For example, when surveying the opinions of teachers, he or she should include them in the problem-solving and action-planning process.

Failing to Recognize Hidden Agendas

Problems can be difficult to solve when action researchers are hampered with *hidden agendas*. For example, if a teacher would like to implement a new curriculum, he or she might encounter resistance from other teachers who want to stay with the current curriculum rather than expend the additional effort in learning the new curriculum.

Treating the Symptom Versus the Cause of the Problem

A common problem of researchers is to *treat the symptom versus the cause of a problem*. The analogy of taking an aspirin for a headache instead of treating the cause of the headache applies action research. Researchers need to remain open-minded when identifying causes for a problem. For example, if an action researcher feels that the best method to address student absenteeism is through training teachers in absenteeism, it will be futile if the root cause of the problem is actually an ineffective school discipline policy (Tomal, 1999).

STEPS IN SOLVING PROBLEMS

Prior to planning and initiating an action, the action researcher must first identify the cause of the problem. There are four basic steps in problem solving (Figure 5.2).

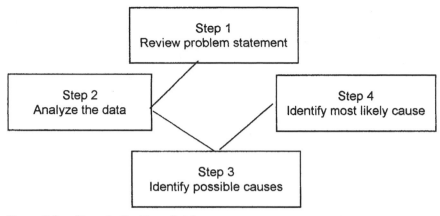

Figure 5.2. Steps in Problem Solving

Review Problem Statement

In step one, it is helpful for the researcher to reexamine the *problem statement* in order to keep focused upon the objective. For example, if a teacher is experiencing a significant upsurge in disciplinary problems in the classroom (i.e., the problem statement), the teacher needs to analyze the data from this perspective.

Analyze the Data

Step two entails the researcher *analyzing the data* for the problem. For example, if a teacher is trying to identify the cause of a current discipline problem, he or she could start by examining differences from past disciplinary problems. The teacher could identify differences, such as gender, class grade, frequency of each disciplinary offense, and degree of misbehavior. The teacher might identify the "what is" versus the "what is not." For example, the "what is" could be identified as predominantly freshman and sophomore girls who are fighting versus junior and senior boys (the "what is not"). In this manner, the teacher can better analyze the data to discern the problem by pinpointing the actual facts to a disciplinary situation.

Identify Possible Causes

In step three, the teacher should list the *possible causes* of the problem. For example, the teacher might benefit from conducting a brainstorming session with his or her colleagues. This collaborative approach could be effective in identifying a multiplicity of potential causes to the problem.

Identifying Most Likely Cause(s)

After the teacher has listed all the possible problems, he or she should then identify the *most likely cause(s)*. In step four, the teacher actually completes the problem-solving phase of the process. There might also be more than one cause of the problem, in which case the teacher should write down the actual causes and rank them in terms of priority.

MANAGING CHANGE

Without a doubt, the most important step to action research is *planning and taking action*. Without taking action, there can be no action research. The essence of action research is to implement meaningful actions that can solve the problem, which always involves change. Therefore, basic to taking action is the need for an action researcher to understand the change process. Whether the change involves students, teachers, parents, or the community, there are several natural resistances to change (Figure 5.3).

Threat to Security

A common resistance to change for some people is the inherent feeling that any deviation from the status quo will result in a personal loss. For example, if a teacher has been teaching at the first-grade level for several years and then is asked to teach at the middle-school level, feelings of failure or inadequacy could occur.

- Threat to security
- Fear of the unknown
- Lack of understanding
- Desire for status quo
- Potential loss of power

Figure 5.3.   Resistance to Change

Fear of the Unknown

Similar to the feeling of insecurity is the fear of not knowing what the new change will bring. For example, if an administrator is considering an extensive restructuring of a school district, the teachers and staff will naturally feel apprehensive about how the change will affect them. They might feel that the benefits will not outweigh the risks of the change.

Lack of Understanding

The threat to security is often compounded when people have a *lack of understanding* of the change effort. This lack of understanding might result from not having sufficient information or control over the change process. Change can create stress in people when they do not have ownership in the change effort. For example, if a teacher is proposing that students participate in a new type of testing program, the students could develop stress if they don't have a thorough understanding of the procedures for the new testing program.

Desire for Status Quo

People can be creatures of habit. If people are content with the present situation, they will have little desire to change. Change often requires a degree of initiative and work and people might not want to exert the effort. For example, elementary students often desire routine in their life. Therefore, they naturally resist any changes in classroom procedures.

Potential Loss of Power

If people have an established position of power within the organization, there will be a tendency to resist change because they feel a potential loss of power. This loss of power can occur at many different levels. For example, a department chairperson would feel a loss of power if his or her position would be eliminated and the person would be required to go back to strictly teaching. Likewise, a student might feel that his or her power is threatened if he or she has been acting as a group leader in a cooperative learning program and the teacher desires to eliminate this program. In both cases, the loss of power can threaten their security and they might resent any change effort.

When planning the action step, the action researcher must understand the basic steps to initiating change (Figure 5.4). Following these basic steps can help ensure that the change process will be successful.

1. **Communicate Purpose** One of the surest ways to undermine a change effort is to fail to make the purpose of change clear. People need to have a logical, well-defined reason for the change. For example, if an administrator is considering making an organization-wide school change, he or she would need to hold several meetings with the staff to explain the purpose of the change, the benefits of the change, and how the change will affect everyone. The administrator might also consider providing a written explanation to all stakeholders (e.g., students, teachers, parents, staff, and community

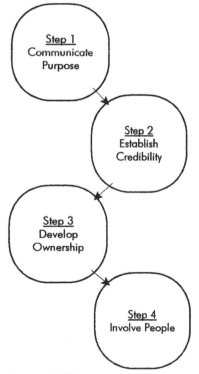

Figure 5.4.   Steps for Successful Change

members) about the proposed change effort. The change agent can seldom ever provide too much communication regarding the purpose of the change. The best rule is to provide more information than you feel is necessary to ensure that everyone has a thorough understanding of the change effort.

2. **Establish Credibility** There cannot be a lack of respect or trust in the initiator of the change effort. One of the best ways to overcome resistance to change is to provide good leadership. If people feel confident with the leader's skills, then the chances for success will be improved. For example, if a teacher is considering implementing a new curriculum program, he or she might obtain the endorsement of one of the respected colleagues to help promote the change effort.

3. **Develop Ownership** Once people have a clear understanding of the purpose of the change and feel there is credibility in leadership, the next step is to ensure that everyone has a feeling of ownership in the change effort. If people feel a personal ownership in the change effort, they will likely be more willing to be actively involved in the change process.

4. **Involve People in the Change Effort** Involving people in the change effort is the last step. Although not all people will want to be involved, the action researcher should try to include as many people as possible. Also, the more people that are involved in the change effort, the more likely others will want to participate.

PLANNING AND INITIATING ACTION

Once the action researcher has considered the conditions for successful change, he or she must plan and initiate the action. For example, if an administrator has conducted an action research study and plans to initiate a school-wide change effort, he or she needs to communicate the purpose of the change, establish credibility, and then involve people in the change effort. The change effort will require the involvement of all stakeholders, such as teachers, administrators, students, board members, parents, and community members. The administrator might first begin by working with a steering committee made up of various stakeholder representatives, such as a teacher, administrator, board member, parent, union representative, and a community member. The purpose of the committee would be to help develop the action plan; provide inspiration, credibility, and direction for the school-wide change effort; help overcome any potential roadblocks; and provide resource support (e.g., finances, materials, facilities, and time). The committee might begin the first phase by developing a clear vision statement for the action to be taken. The vision statement might represent a crystalized long-range picture of what should be accomplished at the school. The vision statement could act as a foundation for the ongoing process to help maintain a central focus while implementing the change effort (Tomal, 1999).

After the mission statement has been established, the steering committee might develop the statement into a school improvement plan (SIP). Once the SIP is complete, the committee might want to ensure that everyone understands the intended change effort by conducting "awareness sessions." This communication effort can be a crucial component to ensure that everyone understands the action, expectations, and their respective roles in accomplishing the action plans.

The next step in initiating the school-wide improvement plan might be the formation of quality teams consisting of stakeholder representatives that could work on the organizational issues. The quality teams could work on such areas as multiculturalism, facilities, security, student achievement, discipline, parent and community relations, and technology. All team members could be trained in team work and group facilitation to improve their effectiveness.

The teams could also consist of stakeholders who genuinely desire to work on school-improvement issues or are associated with the defined issue by nature of their work responsibilities. For example, if the issue is to improve discipline, the school disciplinary dean might be involved on this quality team. A list of each team and issue could be posted on a bulletin board where interested participants could sign up. This process would also help to ensure effective communication and reinforce the purpose of the change effort. The administrator might also provide guidelines for the quality teams, which could include voluntary membership, ground rules for conducting meetings, and work goals.

The quality teams could be lead by a facilitator. The role of the facilitator could be to provide timely communications to all members, credibility for the change effort, and help provide reinforcement for the team's good performance. The facilitator can also keep the teams on task, develop meeting agendas and minutes, and act as communication link with the steering committee and stakeholders. The actual implementation of the actions could also be accomplished through the efforts of the quality teams. The administrator should not implement the school-wide change effort by him or herself. Involving other people is essential to promote ownership and to maximize the use of human resources. For example, a discipline team might develop a new discipline program, but the discipline dean might actually implement it. The quality team could monitor the progress and act as a liaison with the steering committee. The team could also be involved later in evaluating the results of the actions (Tomal, 1999).

Education Issue: Low math achievement
➡ *Potential Action:* Cooperative learning program

Education Issue: High discipline problem
➡ *Potential Action:* New discipline program

Education Issue: Low science achievement
➡ *Potential Action:* Problem-based learning

Education Issue: Learning difficulties
➡ *Potential Action:* Collaborative learning program

Education Issue: Low motivation
➡ *Potential Action:* Motivational rewards program

Education Issue: Low student morale
➡ *Potential Action:* Self-esteem program

Education Issue: Low attendance
➡ *Potential Action:* New attendance policy

Education Issue: High teacher stress
➡ *Potential Action:* Stress management program

Education Issue: Stress and student conflict
➡ *Potential Action:* Parent mediation program

Education Issue: Poor reading skills
➡ *Potential Action:* Home reading program

Figure 5.5.   Methods of Implementing Action

The many methods of implementing actions depend on the nature of the problem (Figure 5.5). The process of initiating action in the classroom is not as elaborate as implementing school-wide change. However, the teacher should consider the conditions for successful change when implementing classroom action. For example, if a teacher is considering the use of a cooperative learning program to improve math learning, he or she might want to consult other teachers who have utilized the program to understand the best method for success. Likewise, the teacher should explain the purpose cooperative learning program to the students, highlighting potential for success and how the program will be implemented.

6

EVALUATING ACTION RESEARCH

AREAS FOR EVALUATION

The final step in taking action is to evaluate the results. Without the evaluation step, the action researcher never knows if the results of the action were successful or if the problem has been resolved. Depending upon the action researcher topic, several areas could be evaluated (Figure 6.1).

Impact on Student Learning

At the core of action research for education is the impact of actions on student learning. One of the central goals of education is to improve student learning. Therefore, this area should be assessed. The assessment of student learning can be accomplished through many methods, such as structured tests, portfolios, performance activities, observations, and informal evaluations. For example, if a teacher implemented graphic calculators to improve mathematical comprehension, the use of problem-based tests could indicate change in learning.

Impact on Student Behavior

The behavior of students is directly related to student performance. Misbehaving students generally do not obtain optimum learning and are

- Impact on student learning
- Impact on student behavior
- Impact on school climate
- Cost benefit of action
- Feasability/utility of action
- Accuracy and effectiveness of action

Figure 6.1.   Areas for Evaluation

disruptive to the learning of other students. For example, several methods of assessing student behavior include: number of disciplinary offenses, student motivation, level of morale, self-esteem, cooperativeness, socialization, group interaction, and amount of time on-task versus off-task behavior.

Impact on School Climate

The use of action research is especially suitable for initiating improvement in school climate. School climate consists of such factors as morale, motivation, spirit, commitment to the school, teamwork, and overall self-esteem. The methods to assess school climate could be undertaken through use of a climate survey or direct observation.

Cost Benefit of Action

Although the actions might be deemed successful, the benefits might not outwiegh the cost of the actions. The benefits must justify the financial resources expended. For example, if an administrator has initiated an action plan of increasing the number of teachers per students as a pilot study for learning for a specified grade level, the amount of financial resources in obtaining additional teachers might not outweigh the benefits of the increased learning and might be cost-prohibitive.

Feasibility and Utility of Action

Another area to evaluate in action research is the feasibility and utility of the actions. *Utility* refers to the timeliness and usefulness of the action while *feasibility* pertains to the appropriateness of the action to the educational environment. Factors impacting utility and feasibility include the total resources needed to implement the action (human, financial, equipment, materials, etc.).

Accuracy and Effectiveness of Action

Another consideration in assessing actions includes the *effectiveness of the action*. If the initial assessment of an action suggests that there has been student improvement in learning, care must be exercised to ensure that the learning is truly meaningful on a long-term basis. For example, a thorough evaluation might reveal that the action has only short-term effects and, therefore, is not reliable. Likewise, if there appears to be improvement in student learning, multiple assessments might need to be executed to determine if the action truly caused improvement or it was the result of simply chance, inaccurate data collection, or invalid interpretation. Given that action research is not an exact science, there is a high threat of personal bias in interpreting the effectiveness of the action taken.

METHODS FOR EVALUATING RESULTS

The action researcher can use many methods to evaluate the effectiveness of actions. An evaluation process that could be undertaken for a school-wide change effort might include the use of quality teams and stakeholders in evaluating results of the entire change effort. Follow-up surveys, individual and group interviews, student academic assessment, feasibility studies, cost-benefit analyses, and benchmarking comparisons can all be part of the process.

One key to understanding the evaluation component of action research is the concept that this research is often a cyclical process. French and Bell (1995) state that "action research is a sequence of events and activities. . . . and it is a cycle of iterations of these activities, sometimes treating the same problem through several cycles and sometimes moving to different problems in each cycle" (p. 139). Therefore, action research is often considered as a method of continuous improvement for an organization. For example, an organizational survey might be used as the intervention method for conducting action research to improve a school district. This same organizational survey could be used over and over again to assess the results of actions in attempting to make continuous improvements.

Lastly, part of the evaluation process should include the distribution of rewards for people who contributed to improvements. People could be awarded for their efforts and achievements through various intrinsic and extrinsic reward systems, such as t-shirts, buttons, certificates, and luncheons. The key to reinforcing successful action research is to ensure that the participants are rewarded for their actual contributions. Celebrating the successes of action research can be a powerful stimulator in making continuous improvements and undertaking additional research studies.

7

CONDUCTING ACTION RESEARCH

SAMPLE RESEARCH STUDY

The purpose of this chapter is to provide an example of a published action research study and to describe the components within the action research model.

STUDY TITLE: COLLABORATIVE PROCESS INTERVENTION: AN ACTION RESEARCH STUDY

Stage 1: Problem Statement/Initial Diagnosis

The study presents the problem statement indicating that the school was on the verge of an educational crisis and was experiencing low teacher morale, conflict, mediocre student test scores, high disciplinary incidents, poor facilities, and instructional materials.

Stage 2: Data Collection

The method of collecting data consisted of an organizational survey and examination of student test scores from the Iowa Test of Basic Skills of Reading and Total Math.

Stage 3: Analysis/Feedback

The analysis consisted of establishing a benchmark of the student tests based upon the Iowa Test of Basic Skills of Reading and Total Math as well as the mean scores from the organizational survey, which consisted of items such as staff morale, school facilities, instructional programs, fiscal management, etc. The feedback process involved reporting the results of the survey to the stakeholders (e.g., educators, parents, and community members).

Stage 4: Action Planning

The action planning process consisted of forming quality teams (e.g., multicultural, policies, student achievement, and safety) in which action plans were developed.

Stage 5: Implementation

The action plans were implemented, which included an extended school day, multicultural events, staff development, improved school policies, upgrading school facilities, and new instructional programs.

Stage 6: Evaluation and Follow Up

An evaluation of the results of the actions included improved test scores (Iowa Test of Basic Skills—overall reading, 3.5%, total math, 1%), and improved staff morale, school facilities, instructional programs, fiscal management, and decreased student disciplinary incidents and crime based upon a follow-up organizational survey, observations, and test analyses.

COLLABORATIVE PROCESS INTERVENTION: AN ACTION RESEARCH STUDY

Daniel R. Tomal
Concordia University River Forest

ABSTRACT

This action research study presents an overview of a *Collaborative Process Intervention (CPI)* used in initiating school-wide change for an elementary school in northeast Illinois. This school, on the verge of an educational crisis, was experiencing problems, such as low teacher and staff morale, conflict, mediocre student test scores, disciplinary problems, budgetary concerns, and inadequate instructional programs.

The CPI strategy consisting of five action research phases—(planning, assessing, executing, implementing, and evaluating) was utilized. It integrated the use of visioning, benchmarking, survey feedback, quality teams, scoreboarding, reward structures, continuous improvement, and other techniques.

Quality teams (e.g., Multicultural, Policies, Student Achievement, Parent and Community Relations, and School Improvement Plan, were used). Actions implemented included: improved student remediation program, multicultural events, staff development, policies, facility upgrading, new instructional and curriculum programs, and changed leadership and teachers, etc.

Results included improved test scores (Iowa Tests of Basic Skills: Overall Reading 3.5%, and Total Math 1%), and improved teacher and staff morale, increased parent and community involvement, reduced conflict and discipline problems; and improved facilities, fiscal management, leadership, and instructional and curriculum programs. Limitations included: lack of administrative commitment, limited time, and use of political agendas. However, the CPI strategy offered a viable approach in making school-wide changes and improvements.

INTRODUCTION

Schools have been faced with a myriad of challenges in recent years. The need to improve student achievement, attendance, discipline, safety and security, multiculturalism, leadership, fiscal management, technology, and a student-centered learning environment are but a few of the ongoing concerns of today's educational institutions. Although educational leaders have utilized various organizational models and school-improvement plans (SIPs), they have often fallen short of expectations in providing meaningful institutional change (Sergiovanni, 1996).

A variety of intervention strategies have been used by educational consultants to help guide schools through the change process (French & Bell, 1995). One such intervention is called the *Collaborative Process Intervention (CPI)*, which has been developed by the author and has been utilized. This strategy focuses on making meaningful organizational improvements through the collaborative efforts of all stakeholders (e.g., teachers, administrators, students, board members, parents, and community members) through shared decision making. The CPI strategy is based upon taking an action-research approach in identifying issues in need of improvement through a systematic process of data collection, and then taking actions to address the issues.

CONTEXT OF STUDY

Statement of the Problem

This action research study was undertaken at an elementary school in northeastern Illinois. The school had more than 600 students from early childhood through eighth grade. The students represented diverse ethnic groups with a large population of Hispanics and African Americans. The staff consisted of about seventy-five employees, such as teachers, administrators, a nurse, psychologists, a social worker, a speech pathologist, a security officer, clerks, and custodians.

The school had recently experienced a significant number of problems, such as poor teacher morale, mediocre student test scores, an increase in disciplinary incidents, inefficient fiscal operations, lack of instructional materials, poor facilities, parent and community complaints, conflict among the teachers, and an upsurge in student crime. The principal had also resigned and an interim principal was assigned to the school until a permanent principal could be hired. Therefore, based upon these problems, the CPI strategy was undertaken by the research consultant to identify the root causes of the school's problems and to make organizational improvements.

Method and Procedures

The CPI strategy consisted of a five-phase process of planning, assessing, executing, implementing, and evaluating. It entailed a comprehensive step-by-step process in working with all stakeholders of the school in bringing about meaningful change within the organization.

Phase One: Planning This first phase began with the research consultant working with a steering committee (consisting of various stakeholder representatives, such as teachers, administrators, board members, parents, union representatives, and community members). The purpose of this committee was to understand the entire CPI process, provide inspiration and direction for the school change, overcome roadblocks, and provide resource support (e.g., finances, materials, facilities, and time).

The first goal of this phase was to develop a clear Vision Statement that reflected the needs of the students. This Vision Statement represented a crystallized long-range picture of what should be accomplished at the school (Daresch, 1995). The development of the Vision Statement required the use of several team building sessions to reduce conflict and build interpersonal relationships and trust among the team members. The Vision Statement became the foundation for the ongoing process and helped everyone maintain a central focus while making educational decisions.

After the Vision Statement had been established, the Steering Committee next developed this statement into a Vision Plan, which included general mission statements, organizational goals that were aligned with district and state goals and outcomes, and a description of the CPI strategy. This Vision Plan also outlined the strategy in developing and implementing the School Improvement Plan.

Once the Vision Plan was completed, the Committee scheduled "awareness sessions" with all stakeholders to communicate the overall plan. Letters describing the Vision Plan were also sent to all stakeholders. This communication process was a crucial component in ensuring that everyone understood the collaborative process, expectations, and their respective roles in accomplishing the goals and objectives.

Phase Two: Assessing The purpose of Phase Two was to clearly identify the organization's strengths and areas in need of improvement (i.e., the major educational problems and issues faced by the school). Assessment areas included curriculum and instruction, safety and security, communications, morale, technology, student transportation, facilities and resources, student centeredness, work responsibilities, student performance, leadership and staff development, and parent and community involvement. This information was collected through organizational surveys, employee interviews, and analysis of student test scores (Greenberg & Baron, 1995).

An overall report (i.e., the strengths and areas in need of improvement) was prepared for the entire school. A copy was also given to the District office. The research consultant attempted to ensure anonymity and openness among the respondents. Some of the general areas in need of improvement included: leadership, school policies and procedures, communications, organizational climate, curriculum and instruction, educational resources, teacher committees, parent-community involvement, building facilities, school temperature, multicultural appreciation, administrative and organizational structure, and school budget and allocation of funds.

Once the reports were prepared, a series of "feedback sessions" were held for all stakeholders. The feedback sessions allowed everyone to understand the results of the assessment, clarify issues, and ask questions about the process. An overview of the next step in the CPI process concluded the feedback sessions.

As part of the organizational assessment, benchmarking, a process of identifying the best practices of other schools, was used as a basis for achieving greater performance (Camp, 1989). The benchmarking process was conducted by a team of teachers.

Although the benchmarking process could have been done continuously throughout the school year, the identification of suitable educational programs was used specifically to establish goals for the School Improvement Plan and find suitable actions to address the more immediate issues facing the school.

Phase Three: Executing To address the improvement areas identified in the assessing phase, quality teams were formed in Phase Three. These teams consisted of concerned stakeholders, such as teachers, administrators, staff, parents, and community members who were willing to work on a team in addressing areas in need of improvement in the school.

There were several teams established in such areas as Policies, Multiculturalism, Facilities, Student Achievement, School

Improvement, Parent and Community Relations, Safety, Human Resources and Organizational Development, and Technology. About six-to-ten members were on each team. Each team was responsible for addressing a specific issue as established in Phase Two. All teams were trained in team building and group problem-solving and decision-making strategies. Each quality team consisted of various stakeholders who genuinely desired to work on an issue, or who were associated with an issue by nature of their work responsibilities. For example, if the issue was to improve discipline, the school disciplinary dean was involved on this quality team. A listing of each team and issue was posted on a bulletin board where interested candidates could also sign up.

Some general guidelines for the quality teams included: voluntary membership, ground rules for conducting the meetings, and clearly stated team goals and outcomes. For example, the Achievement Team was given the task of addressing student academic deficiencies. Various actions were proposed and implemented, such as an extended-day school program, improved curriculum and instruction, and acquisition of additional resources (e.g., books, materials) for students with academic deficiencies. In addition to establishing quality teams, a pool of facilitators was selected. These facilitators were various stakeholders who were trained in group-processing techniques. The facilitators were to act as group leaders in facilitating the sessions and were not to be viewed as chairpersons of a committee. They kept the quality teams on task, developed the meeting agendas and minutes, and acted as a communication link with the Steering Committee and school (Harrington, 1987). The facilitators also posted their teams' minutes on the school bulletin board so that everyone could be kept informed on the teams' progress—a process called "scoreboarding." In most cases, facilitators were assigned to a team that was not closely associated with the members of the team or the issue. Thus, the facilitators could remain neutral and maintain a focus on facilitating the session, not get involved with the issue. The overall goal of the facilitator was to assist the teams in solving problems and making decisions by consensus.

RESULTS

Phase Four: Implementing Upon approval by the Steering Committee, the action plans were implemented. The quality teams were not necessarily responsible for actually implementing the action plans. A quality team, in many cases, worked with the appropriate individual or department to implement the action plan. For example, the Policies Team developed a program for improving student attendance, but an administrator actually implemented it. The quality team stayed "on the sidelines," monitored the progress, acted as a liaison with the Steering Committee, assisted the administrator, and helped manage the process.

As result of the quality teams' efforts significant actions were implemented. For example, the Policies Team developed and implemented several disciplinary policies, school rules and procedures, and parent and teacher handbooks. The Multicultural Team implemented many programs to celebrate the diverse cultures of the school. Safety programs were implemented, community members became more involved, school facilities improved, and conflict decreased. A follow-up survey also showed significant improvement in morale within the school.

Although it was too early to assess the long-term effects of the school changes on student achievement, initial test scores should increase. Scores on the Iowa Tests of Basic Skills indicated an overall improvement of 3.2% in Reading Comprehension, and 1% in Total Math—a nice change from the previous downward trend. The school's principal, working with the Human Resources and Organizational Development team, made several improvements in fiscal operations, staff and office changes, staff development programs, and other organizational areas (Tomal, 1993).

Phase Five: Evaluating Upon implementation of the action plan, the quality teams worked with the appropriate teams in evaluating the results of the actions. Follow-up surveys, individual and group interviews, student academic assessments, and benchmarking comparisons were all a part of the process. The teams were rewarded for their efforts and achievements. Various extrinsic rewards systems, such as t-shirts, buttons, certificates, and luncheons were used. The teachers were also paid for their extended-school day through State Chapter One funds. Most importantly, the achievements of the students were celebrated through school events. Recognizing the students and including parents and community through school events resulted in personal satisfaction and motivation for continued success.

As a result of the actions, selected quality teams continued their work on achieving continuous improvement. The continuous improvement process entailed the constant pursuit of quality improvement in all aspects of the organization (Ciampa, 1992). The quality teams re-examined the teams' action plans and suggested ways for even better improvement.

The final step involved re-assessing the entire CPI strategy and making necessary improvements to the process. The Steering Committee rotated members to include fresh viewpoints and allowed others to participate in the process at this level.

DISCUSSION

Although the CPI strategy offers a viable approach in achieving school improvement, a myriad of problems can occur. In this study, problems included lack of quality time for team meetings, negative attitudes by teachers and staff, lack of administrative support to teachers and staff, infiltration of political agendas by stakeholders, poor attendance by team members, and lack of financial support.

The inherent distrust between teachers and administrators needed to be overcome in order to establish the process. Many teachers were skeptical about the process and the principal's commitment to teachers and the process. Although team building and conflict resolution sessions helped to reduce this problem, there continued to be some conflict and mistrust.

Variations of the CPI strategy can easily be adapted for an organization based upon its unique needs and characteristics. Although the process can be useful in developing the SIP for the ensuing year, it can also be valuable as an intervention process at any point in the school year. Schools that are in an educational crisis or are experiencing acute or chronic educational problems and do not know what to do can utilize the process as a catalyst to initiate viable change. For example, if a school is suddenly put on probation, the process could be utilized to reassess the school, develop a revised SIP, and implement the modified plan.

Every organization is a living organism unto itself and the CPI strategy, like any process, will need to be tailored for the individual school. Roadblocks will undoubtedly be encountered and the educational leader and school consultant will need to be able to adjust the process. However, the use of the CPI strategy can offer a practical and viable approach in establishing and bringing about meaningful organizational change and long-term school improvement.

REFERENCES

Bracey, G. (1994). The fourth Bracey report on the condition of public education. *Phi Delta Kappan, 76*, 114–127.

Camp, R. (1989). *Benchmarking*. White Plains, NY: ASQC Quality Press.

Ciampa, D. (1992). *Total quality: A user's guide for implementation*. New York: Addison-Wesley Publishing.

Cuban, L. (1994). How can a national strategy miss a third of our schools? *Education Digest, 59*, 12–17.

Daresch, J. & Playko, M. (1995). *Supervision as a proactive process*. Prospect Heights, IL: Waveland Press.

French, W. & Bell, C. (1995). *Organization development*. Englewood Cliffs, NJ: Prentice Hall.

Greenberg, J. & Baron, R. (1995). *Behavior in organizations*. Needham Heights, MA: Allyn & Bacon.

Harrington, J. (1987). *The improvement process*. New York: McGraw-Hill.

Kossen, S. (1994). *The human side of organizations*. New York: Harper-Collins.

Lewis, J. (1986). *Achieving excellence in our schools*. Westbury, NY: Wilkerson.

Sergiovanni, T. (1996). *Leadership for the schoolhouse*. San Francisco: Jossey-Bass.

Tanner, D. (1993). A nation truly at risk. *Phi Delta Kappan, 75*, 288–297.

Tomal, D. (1993). Staff development, filling gaps in teacher preparation. *The School Administrator, 50* (2), 51.

Tomal, D. (1992). Self management theory for developing teacher effectiveness: a new pedagogic approach to teacher effectiveness. *The Teacher Educator, 28* (2), 51.

Tomal, D. (1998). Collaborative process intervention: an action research study. Critical issues in teacher education. *Journal of the Association of Teacher Educators, 7*, 53–60.

Appendix A

ETHICAL STANDARDS OF THE AMERICAN EDUCATIONAL RESEARCH ASSOCIATION

II. GUIDING STANDARDS: RESEARCH POPULATIONS, EDUCATIONAL INSTITUTIONS, AND THE PUBLIC

A. Preamble

Educational researchers conduct research within a broad array of settings and institutions, including schools, colleges, universities, hospitals, and prisons. It is of paramount importance that educational researchers respect the rights, privacy, dignity, and sensitivies of their research populations and also the integrity of the institutions within which the research occurs.

Educational researchers should be especially careful in working with children and the vulnerable populations. These standards are intended to reinforce and strengthen already existing standards enforced by institutional review boards and other professional associations.

B. Standards

1. Participants, or their guardians, in a research study have the right to be informed about the likely risks involved in the research and of potential consequences for participants, and to give their informed

consent before participating in research. Educational researchers should communicate the aims of the investigation as well as possible to informants and participants (and their guardians), and appropriate representatives of institutions, and keep them updated about any significant changes in the research program.

2. Honesty should characterize the relationship between researchers and participants and appropriate institutional representatives. Deception is discouraged; it should be used only when clearly necessary for scientific studies, and should then be minimized. After the study the researcher should explain to the participants and institutional representatives the reasons for the deception.

3. Educational researchers must be sensitive to any locally established institutional policies or guidelines for conducting research.

4. Participants have the right to withdraw from the study at any time, unless otherwise constrained by their official capacities or roles.

5. Educational researchers should exercise caution to ensure that there is no exploitation for personal gain of research populations or of institutional settings of research. Educational researchers should not use their influence over subordinates, students, or others to compel them to participate in research.

6. Researchers have a responsibility to be mindful of cultural, religious, gender, and other significant differences within the research population in the planning, conduct, and reporting of their work.

7. Researchers should carefully consider and minimize the use of research techniques that might have negative social consequences, for example, experimental interventions that might deprive students of important parts of the standard curriculum.

8. Educational researchers should be sensitive to the integrity of ongoing institutional activities and alert appropriate institutional representatives of possible disturbances in such activities which may result from the conduct of the research.

9. Educational researchers should communicate their findings and the practical significance of their research in clear, straightforward, and appropriate language to relevant research populations, institutional representatives, and other stakeholders.

10. Informants and participants have a right to remain anonymous. This right should be respected when no clear understanding to the contrary has been reached. Researchers are responsible for taking appropriate precautions to protect the confidentiality of both participants and data. Those being studied should be made aware of the capacities of the various data-gathering technologies to be used in the investigation so that they can make an informed decision about their participation. It should also be made clear to informants and participants that despite every effort made to preserve it, anonymity may be compromised. Secondary researchers should respect and maintain the anonymity established by primary researchers.

Used with permission from the American Educational Research Association, 2002.

Appendix B

SEVENTY-FIVE IDEAS FOR CONDUCTING ACTION RESEARCH

1. Improving students' reading through parent interaction
2. Improving gender appreciation through coeducational classrooms
3. Creating prolific readers through the use of literature circles
4. Implementing strategies for discipline improvement
5. Improving female mathematical ability through heterogeneous educational programs
6. Improving children's reading through letter recognition
7. Integrating technology in the classroom for learning enhancement
8. Involving parents to improve student learning
9. Investigating year-round school to improve academic achievement
10. Implementing a mentor program to improve teacher effectiveness
11. Increasing student engagement through conversational styles
12. Using accommodations for learning disabled students
13. Improving reading fluency through use of the Great Leaps Reading Program
14. Developing a looping program to improve achievement

15. Improving reading comprehension through intrinsic motivators
16. Using peer mediation to reduce student conflict
17. Using a structured learning program for attention deficit students
18. Improving academic achievement through student-led conferences
19. Improving student learning through peer tutoring techniques
20. Using a multi-age classroom environment to improve student social behaviors
21. Enhancing understanding of algebra through prompt writing and computational problems
22. Improving discipline through student involvement in extracurricular activities
23. Improving student attitudes toward reading through self-selection reading material techniques
24. Improving student self-esteem through a student advisory program
25. Improving student study skills and habits through television viewing preferences
26. Improving basic mathematic skills through remedial programming techniques
27. Improving the teacher evaluation system through benchmarking
28. Improving student homework through parental involvement for gifted students
29. Reducing teacher burnout through mentor intervention
30. Using hypnosis to improve student study skills
31. Using character education to improve discipline
32. Improving attendance through extrinsic motivators
33. Enhancing reading through the use of family reading programs
34. Improving science achievement through hands-on teaching methods
35. Using portfolio assessment to improve student learning
36. Improving mathematic achievement through journal writing
37. Improving student learning through ability grouping
38. Using brain-based learning for teaching effectiveness
39. Improving reading attitudes through the use of literature circles
40. Improving academic achievement through the use of graphic organizers

41. Increasing music ability through improved reading and language skills
42. Using block scheduling to improve scheduling efficiency
43. Using a summer bridge program to improve benchmark grades
44. Using flexible access library media programs to improve student achievement
45. Improving high school drop out rate through mentoring
46. Using multiple intelligences to enhance learning
47. Using an English immersion program for bilingual education improvement
48. Using phonic intervention for ESL student improvement
49. Improving math comprehension through use of journal writing
50. Using keyword mnemonic memorization for learning disabled students
51. Improving technical performance with mental visualization
52. Using sign language instruction to improve early childhood reading readiness skills
53. Improving reading proficiency through self-advocacy motivational tools
54. Improving problem solving and chemistry knowledge through use of didactic teaching techniques
55. Improving student literacy through an after-school newspaper club program
56. Improving discipline through the use of a uniform discipline code program
57. Improving education of learning disabled students through the use of personality style techniques
58. Improving at-risk emergent reading achievement through an early tutoring program
59. Improving reading achievement through an integrated reading program
60. Improving learning through gifted clustering techniques
61. Using direct instructional techniques on reading comprehension
62. Enhancing student responsibility with student-led conferences
63. Improving social studies achievement through cooperative learning
64. Using visual instruction for reading comprehension

65. Improving an intervention program through the use of instructional interest program

66. Repeating oral reading prompts to improve student oral reading fluency

67. Improving second grade student learning through word-attack strategies

68. Using bibliotherapy to grow socially and personally

69. Improving students' spatial-temporal reasoning through piano sonatas

70. Using aerobic exercise to improve children's classroom behavior

71. Improving reading through an accelerated reading program

72. Improving cognitive ability through a think-tank enrichment model

73. Using a dress code to reduce gang presence

74. Using a level system for behavior disorder students

75. Improving athletic performance through cognitive restructuring

BIBLIOGRAPHY

American Educational Research Association. (2002). *Ethical standards of American Educational Research Association.* Washington, DC: AERA.

American Psychological Association (APA). (1992). *Ethical principles of psychologists and code of conduct.* Washington, DC: APA.

Argyris, C. (1970). *Intervention theory and model: A behavioral science.* Reading, MA: Addison-Wesley.

Arhar, J., Holly, J., & Kasten, W. (2001). *Action research for teachers.* New Jersey: Prentice-Hall

Beckhard, R. (1969). *Organizational development: Strategies and models.* Reading, MA: Addison-Wesley.

Bernard, H. (1994). *Research methods in cultural anthropology.* Beverly Hills, CA: Sage.

Camp, R. (1989). *Benchmarking.* White Plains, NY: ASQC Quality Press.

Dewey, J. (1933). *How we think.* New York: Health.

Farr, R., & Tone, B. (1994). *Portfolio and performance assessment.* New York: Harcourt Brace.

French, W. & Bell, C. (1995). *Organization development.* Englewood Cliffs, NJ: Prentice-Hall.

Frick, T., & Semmel, M. (1978). Observer agreement and reliabilities of classroom observation measures. *Review of Educational Research*, 48, 157–184.

Gall, M., Borg, W., & Gall, J. (1996). *Educational research.* New York: Longman.

Gay, L. R. (1996). *Educational research: Competencies for analysis and application.* Upper Saddle River, NJ: Merrill/Prentice-Hall.

Grundy, S. (1994). Action research at the school level: Possibilities and problems. *Educational Action Research,* 2(1), 23–36.

Gunz, J. (1996). Jacob L. Moreno and the origins of action research. *Educational Action Research,* 4(1), 145–148.

Hammersley, M. (1993). On the teacher as researcher. *Educational Action Research,* 1(3), 425–441.

Herrington, J. (1987). *The improvement.* New York: McGraw-Hill.

Hoffke, S. E., & Stevenson, R. B. (Eds.). (1995). *Educational action research: Becoming practically critical.* New York: Teacher College Press.

Jung, C. (1923). *Psychological types.* New York: Harmony Books.

Keemis, S., & McTaggert, R. (Eds.) (1988). *The action research planner* (3rd ed.). Geelong, Victoria, Australia: Deakin University Press.

Kennedy, Mary M. (1997). The connection between research and practice. *Educational Researcher:* 26(7), 4–12.

Leedy, P. & Ormrod, J. (2001). *Practical research.* New Jersey: Prentice-Hall.

Lewin, Kurt. (1947) Frontiers in group dynamics. *Human Relations,* 1.2, 143–153.

Maslow, A. (1943). A theory of motivation. *Psychological Review,* 50, 370–396.

Mayo, E. (1939). *The human problems of an industrial civilization.* New York: MacMillan.

McMillan, James H. (1996). *Educational research: Fundamentals for the consumer* (2nd ed.). New York: HarperCollins College Publishers.

Mills, G. (2000). *Action research: A guide for the teacher researcher.* New Jersey: Prentice-Hall.

Piaget, J. (1926). *The language and thought of the child.* New York: Harcourt, Brace, and World.

Sagor, Richard (1992). *How to conduct collaborative action research.* Alexandria, VA: Association for Supervision and Curriculum Development.

Shepard, H. (1960). *An action research model in action research program for organizational improvement.* Ann Arbor: University of Michigan.

Spradley, J. (1980). *Participant observation.* New York: Holt, Rinehart & Winston.

Tomal, D. (1996). Action research: A practical and viable method for educators. *Lutheran Education* 132(2), 88–94.

Tomal, D. (1997). Collaborative process intervention: An action research study. *Critical Issues in Teacher Education* 7, 53–60.

Tomal, D. (1998). Benchmarking: A viable process for discovering the best educational practices. *Eastern Education Journal* 27(1), 36–38.

Tomal, D. (1999). *Discipline by negotiation.* Lancaster, PA: Technomic Publishing.

INDEX

ABOUT THE AUTHOR

Dan Tomal is an associate professor and chair of the Department of Educational Leadership at Concordia University, River Forest, Illinois. He has been a public high school teacher, administrator, corporate vice president, and consultant. He received his B.S. and M.A.E. degrees in education from Ball State University and a Ph.D. in educational administration from Bowling Green State University. He has consulted for numerous schools and organizations and has testified before the United States Congress. While a professor at Purdue University North Central, he was voted the outstanding teacher of year by the faculty and students. He has authored six books and more than fifty articles and research studies. He has made guest appearances on numerous radio and television shows such as: *This Morning* (CBS); *Cover to Cover, Les Brown, Joan Rivers, Tom Snyder* (NBC); *700 Club* (CBN); *ABC News* (ABC); and *Focal Point*, and *Chicago Talks* (WCFC). He is author of the book *Discipline by Negotiations*: *Methods for Managing Student Behavior* (Scarecrow Press, Technomic Books). Dan lives with his wife, Annette Tomal, Ph.D., and their three children in Wheaton, Illinois.